miguel angel rios
walkabout

This catalog is published by the Des Moines Art Center on the occasion of the exhibition *Miguel Angel Ríos: Walkabout*, organized by the Des Moines Art Center.

Library of Congress
Cataloging-in-Publication Data
Ríos, Miguel Angel, 1943 –
Catalog of the exhibition held at the Des Moines Art Center
February 3 – April 22, 2012
ISBN number: 978-1-879003-62-0 (pbk.)
1.Ríos, Miguel Angel, 1943-Exhibitions
I. Vicario, Gilbert II. Des Moines Art Center III. Title
Library of Congress Control Number: 2011945836

Des Moines Art Center
4700 Grand Avenue
Des Moines, Iowa 50312
www.desmoinesartcenter.org

Editor: Gilbert Vicario
Copy Editor: Carrie Schmitz
Translator for Ruth Estévez essay: Sarah Demeuse
Translator for Osvaldo Sánchez essay: Tamara Stuby
Designer: Annabel Wimer Design
Printer: Garner Printing

1,000 copies printed

Cover: *Untitled #8* (*Meta* series), 2010
Inside Cover: *El viaje del botanista* (The Botanist's Journey), 1997–2002

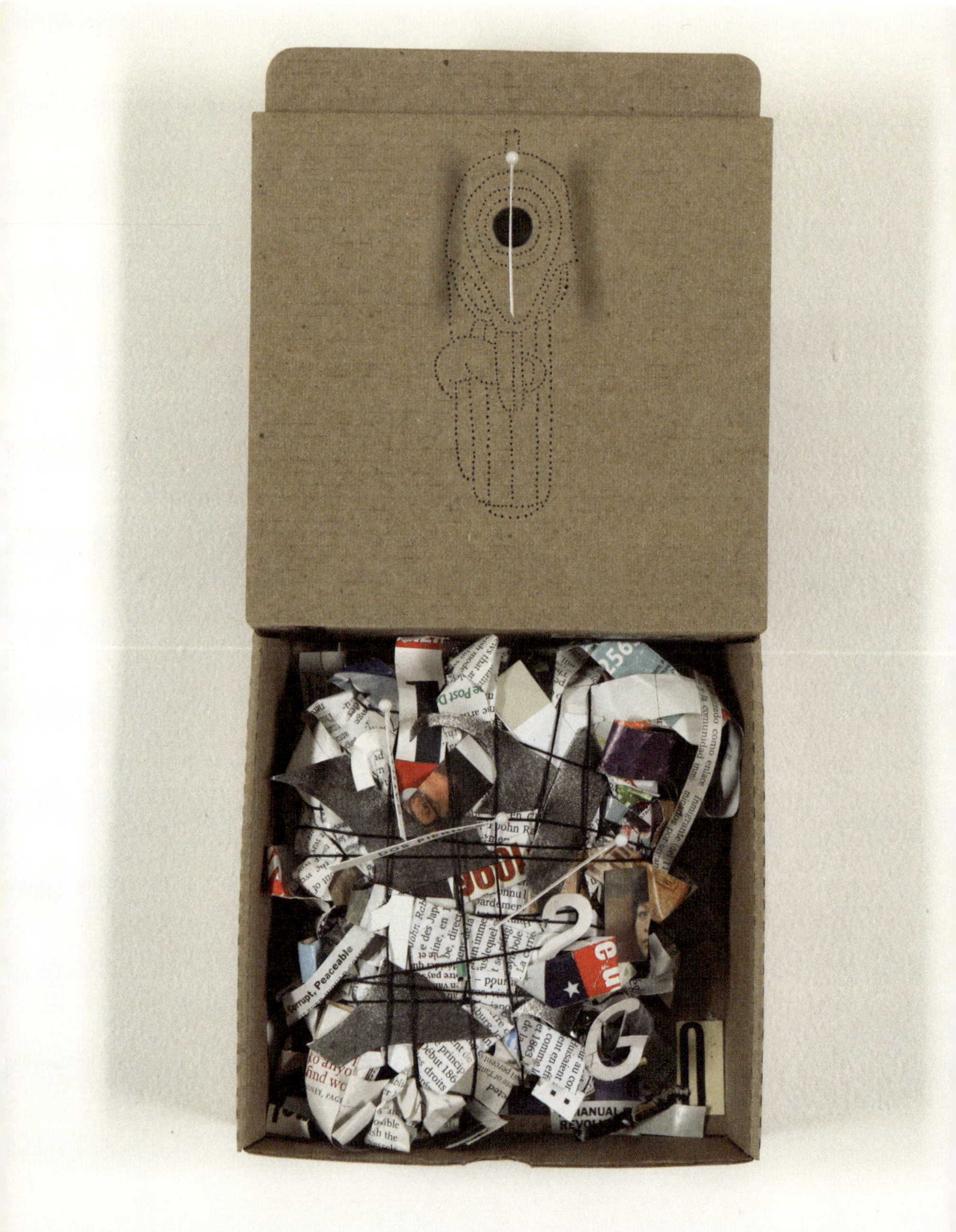

SendEx Box #4, 2011

foreword

Like many, I am enthralled by imaginings of the past. These include views not only of world history, but of my own personal experiences, with which my relationship seems to shift as I grow older. Scrutinizing images or cultural objects from the past as well as the present provides insights into the values of a time. I am especially intrigued by fluctuations in these perceptions—when established beliefs are turned inside out; when the things we have taken for granted are proven to be fabrications. The identity of William Shakespeare, the cause of Vincent van Gogh's death, and the deeds of Christopher Columbus come to mind. In turn, new information gathered from more in-depth explorations of cultural representations has enhanced our appreciation of, for example, the intellectual and cultural sophistication of the indigenous peoples of the Americas at the time of the Spanish conquest. Time and again, we see swings in our assessments of a point in history. This certainly includes our own moment.

Miguel Angel Ríos shares a similar responsiveness to these changes in perception. He was born in Argentina, but he left that country to escape the political turmoil there. After settling in

New York City and then Mexico City, where he maintains studios, he is now exploring his own past and the history of Latin America. Through alternately jarring, poetic, and graceful films, videos, drawings, and collages, Ríos connects the past and the present. His potent mixtures serve as both shifting visions of a personal journey and broader, universal responses to a time and place.

I want to acknowledge and thank Senior Curator Gilbert Vicario for organizing this project. The exhibition continues the Art Center's ongoing investigations into significant art of our time playing out on a global arena. Vicario was ably assisted by Associate Registrar Mickey Koch and Chief Preparator Jay Ewart and his staff. In addition, Ruth Estévez, Julieta González, Raphael Rubinstein, and Osvaldo Sánchez provided insightful essays on the nature of displacement and shifts in perception in relation to Ríos' work. The designer Annabel Wimer combined all of these components together in this noteworthy publication; I thank her for her elegant touch. Lastly, I would like to thank Miguel Angel Ríos for continuing to ask the very human questions: Where do I come from and where do I belong?

Jeff Fleming
Director, Des Moines Art Center

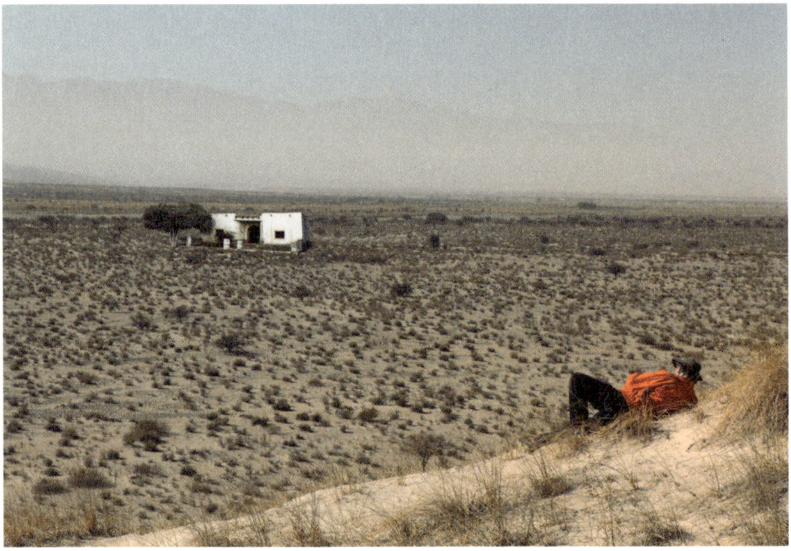

Portrait of Miguel Angel Ríos in San Jose Norte Catamarca, Argentina, 2009. Photo: Carlos Cardenas

introduction

Since 2000, the New York City- and Mexico City-based artist Miguel Angel Ríos has been creating haunting and poetic works in video and mixed media. *Walkabout* presents a selection of five video and multimedia installations along with paintings and works on paper that demonstrate his unique relationship to the South American and Mexican landscape. While much of the work in this show has never before been exhibited, it offers a focused examination of the preoccupations and concerns that have informed Ríos' practice over the last decade. The title of the exhibition invokes the traditional associations to rites of passage, spiritual awakenings, and self-awareness that come from solitary encounters in the desert landscape. In more concrete terms, his relationship to this type of landscape is explored through work that questions long-held preconceptions related to Latin American regionalism and European colonialism in this part of the world. Originally from Catamarca in northern Argentina, Ríos relocated to New York City in the mid-1970s to escape the dire political situation during the military dictatorship in that country. Although Ríos initially spent time in New York, he eventually relocated to Mexico, where he was able to reestablish a connection with Latin America yet keep a safe distance from the political strife in his native country. Through his experience of political dislocation, central themes have emerged, including the exploration of alternate states of mind, struggles of power, and immunity from violence through works executed in a prolific and wide-ranging spectrum of styles and materials.

Those who have followed the artist's career may remember that during the 1980s, much of Miguel Angel Ríos' work focused on delicate handmade objects using low-fired clay and textiles. These compelling objects spoke of indigenous traditions conceptually overlaid with contemporary dialogues on dislocation, politics, and identity. By the mid-1990s, his process morphed into massively scaled works on paper, the *Maps* series, which explored the role of cartography in the colonization of the New World in surprisingly beautiful and technically virtuosic ways. Ríos received critical attention for this body of work that was featured in the exhibition *Mapping*, 1994, at The Museum of Modern Art. However, by the end of the 1990s, as Ríos began to be included in many international exhibitions, he noticed the proliferation of artists using video as their primary means of expression. It was during this time that the artist began to explore the potential of this medium as a means of communicating more directly with his audience. As with Ríos' previous work (sculpture and mixed-media installations), the artist's early video work focuses on the European conquest of Latin America and later moves into more abstract territories related to existentialism, hallucination, and violence.

In the video *Los niños brotan de noche* (The Children Spring Forth from the Night), 2002, Ríos documents his encounter with a female shaman named Doña Gudelia, who guides him through an experience with psychoactive fungi. Filmed almost in total darkness, *Los niños* signals the artist's exploration of indigenous traditions and customs that are completely alien to him yet exist within the same geographic proximity. In the three-channel video installation *Ni me busques ... No me encuentras* (Don't Look for Me ... You Won't Find Me), 2002, he explores the hypnotic power of the desert through his quest to find the mythical peyote cactus used by the Huichol Indians of western-central Mexico. Aside from being technically innovative, *Ni me busques* constituted the most ambitious examination of Ríos' investigation of mind-altering substances using the cinematic medium of video. Toward the later part of the last decade, he has moved away from the utopian and surrealist implications of psychoactive plant materials and shifted into more abstract examinations of the manifestations of power and abuse. This can be clearly seen in a highly successful series of videos depicting spinning black-and-white tops, with the first in that series titled *A Morir* (Till

Death), 2003. In more recent work, the artist has continued his investigation into the nature of violence in characteristic abstract terms in works such as *Mecha* (Fuse), 2010, in which a series of chaotic and menacing scenarios is staged using pyrotechnics, kinetic actions, and gunpowder.

Like *A Morir*, the idea behind *Mecha* began through Ríos' fascination with regional games played in Latin American countries. In Colombia, there is a little-known game called *tejo* played within a small district inside Bogotá. *Tejo*, which roughly translates to the type of wood used in archery, is a game played in teams of six or more men and women with heavy metal disks. Each player throws a disk, or *tejo*, toward a square of wet mud 15 to 20 centimeters deep, trying to hit targets made of pink triangular detonators called *mechas*, which are filled with gunpowder and explode on impact. The video installation combines footage of this game using actors filmed inside a warehouse that resembles a postapocalyptic, industrial landscape containing wire fences that alternately resemble cages or jail cells. While channeling the kinetic metamechanics of the Swiss artist Jean Tinguely, *Mecha* constructs a reality that suggests urban guerilla warfare, drug trafficking in Mexico and Colombia, or the deadly struggle of gang warfare.

Ríos' abiding interest in the isolation of the desert as a site of spiritual renewal and human connection is explored in two recent pieces, *Meta* (Goal), 2009–2010, a sound installation dealing with spatial perception and communication that was recorded in the Andes mountains along the Calchaquí Valley in northern Argentina, where the artist grew up; and *Rooom Rooom*, 2010, a single-channel video related to a game that he played as a child. The game entails attaching a wooden tablet to a cord; when spun, the tablet creates a loud vibration that reverberates throughout the valley. The acoustic characteristics of the region are exceptional due to the proximity of the high mountain walls, thus creating an immense echo chamber. In the artist's updated version of the game, the tablets are wrapped in aluminum foil, and each features an inscription—letters, numbers—indicating specific dates of tragic events in recent world history: NY9-11 (New York City), MAD3-11 (Madrid), OK4-19 (Oklahoma City),

MUN9-05 (Munich), etc.

Running parallel to his multimedia installations is a selection of works on paper and paintings on Masonite that both exemplify and mirror related themes to his video works. Usually they start out as sketchbooks and storyboards for the videos, simple graphite-on-paper illustrations that are quickly laid down. Eventually, the drawings begin to take on lives of their own by becoming textural and formal objects of great beauty and visual depth. *El viaje del botanista* (The Botanist's Journey), 1997–2002, is a monumental installation that poetically documents Ríos' experiments with hallucinogenic plants. Composed of photographs, fax paper, cut paper objects, and more than 65 quickly drawn sketches that illustrate everything from the plants themselves to more elaborate and abstract psychoanalytic renderings of his experiences, *El viaje del botanista* constructs a surreal cartography that seeks to articulate his experience in a chaotic yet visceral way. A related series of paintings with the same title as his video installation *Ni me busques ... No me encuentras* (Don't Look For Me ... You Won't Find Me), 2002, plays with the flatness and horizontality of the desert landscape through the wide-angle frame of the small canvases. Most of them depict the artist in bizarre scenarios with recurring imagery that lends these paintings a proto-cinematic quality.

Rounding out the exhibition is a recent series of drawings/collages that look at the ubiquitous presence of violence in contemporary society, as articulated in his video *Mecha*. These works feature drawings of truncated clusters of handguns, machine gun barrels, and semiautomatic weapons pointed at the viewer. Some feature cardboard constructions of these weapons, along with phrases that are cut into the objects saying, "If you want peace, prepare yourself for war," and "When I hear the word culture I reach for my gun." While others, such as *Untitled (Cut Out Drawing, Large)*, 2011, display these weapons through the use of the perforated-paper folk-art tradition found in Mexico. Running counter to these subjective interpretations of violence are his white cut-paper constructions from the *Meta* series. These are poetic, visual representations of sound as vortexlike shapes that seemingly jump out of the two-dimensional plane of the paper. *Untitled (Meta 1/2)* and *Untitled (Meta 2/2)*, 2011, feature the profile of the artist yelling into these cones, while others feature randomly placed numerical markings used for measurements on rulers or tape measures. Ultimately, the works lament the lack of communication in an age of social media and information technology through the very humble technology of the paper collage. These, like the other works on paper in the exhibition, are integrated alongside the video installations to demonstrate the importance of artistic process in Ríos' work and also to create an intermedia discourse between video image and object. Although Ríos is quite skilled at producing and directing video installations at this point, the works on paper demonstrate his unerring faith in the handmade object and its ability to coexist in a world dominated by the electronic image. *Walkabout* seeks to explore these aspects as it presents a rare glimpse of an artistic vision at the crossroads of tradition and innovation.

Gilbert Vicario
Senior Curator, Des Moines Art Center

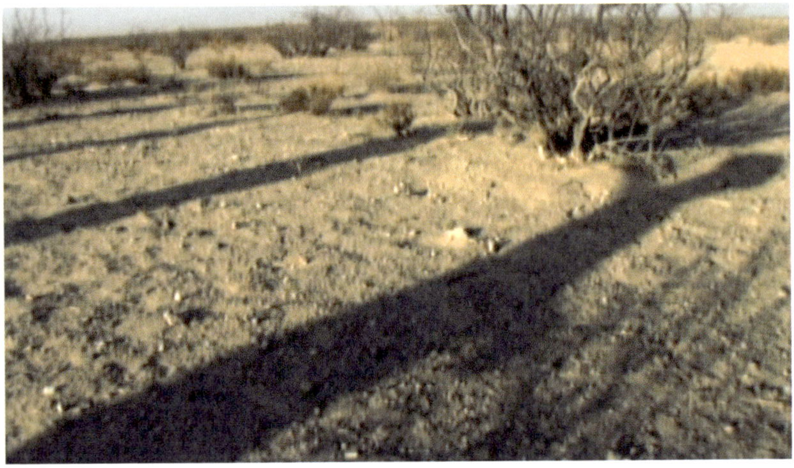

Rooom, Rooom, 2010 (video still)

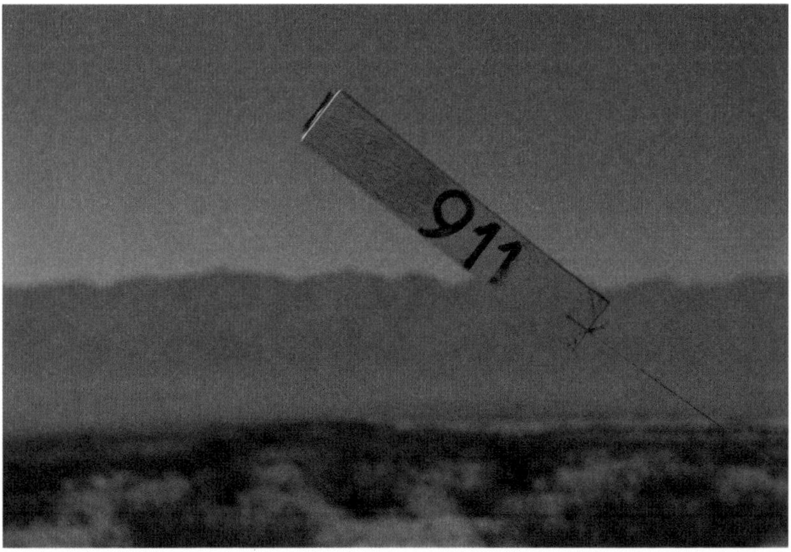

Rooom, Rooom, 2010 (video still)

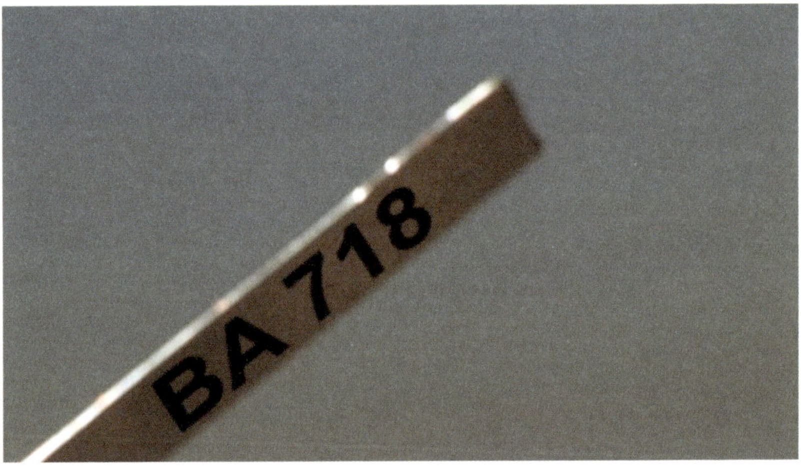

Preceding page and this page: *Rooom, Rooom*, 2010 (video still)

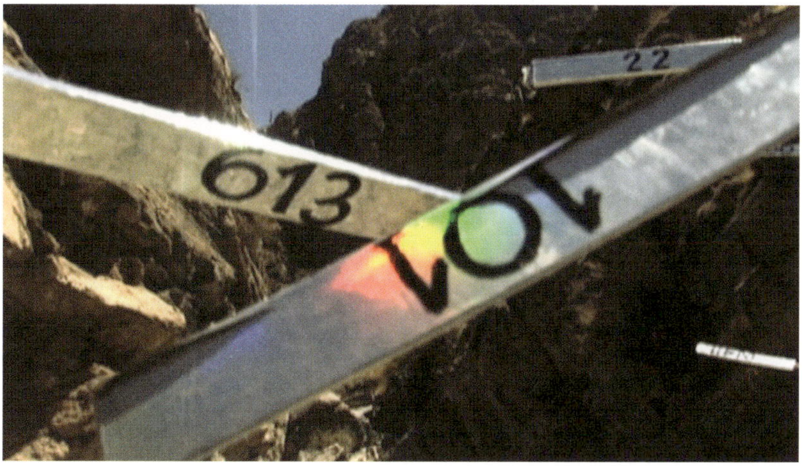

Rooom, Rooom, 2010 (video still)

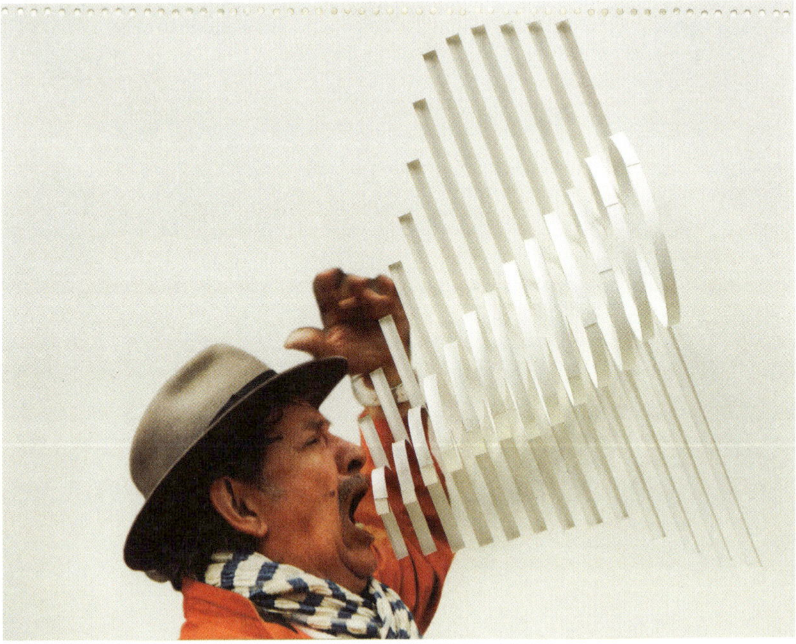

Untitled (Meta 1/2), 2011

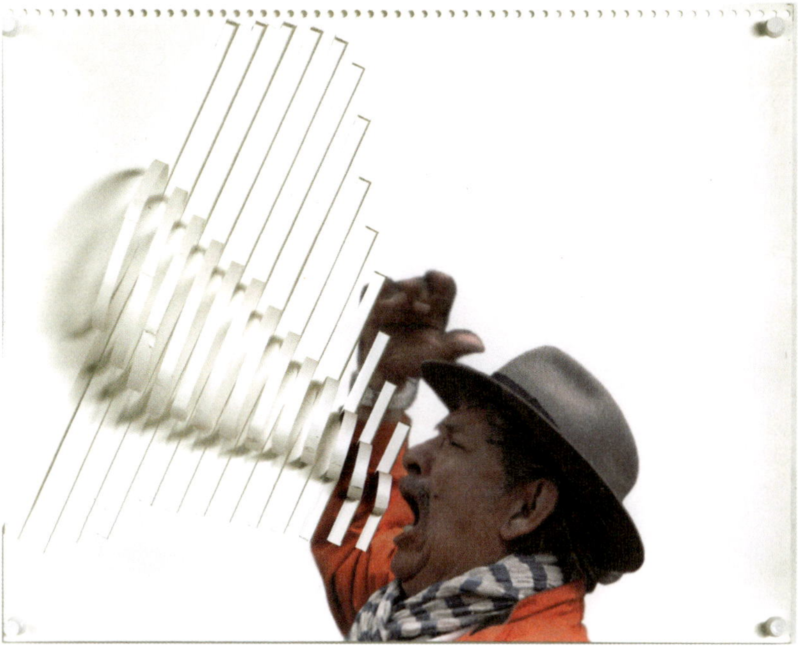

Untitled (Meta 2/2), 2011

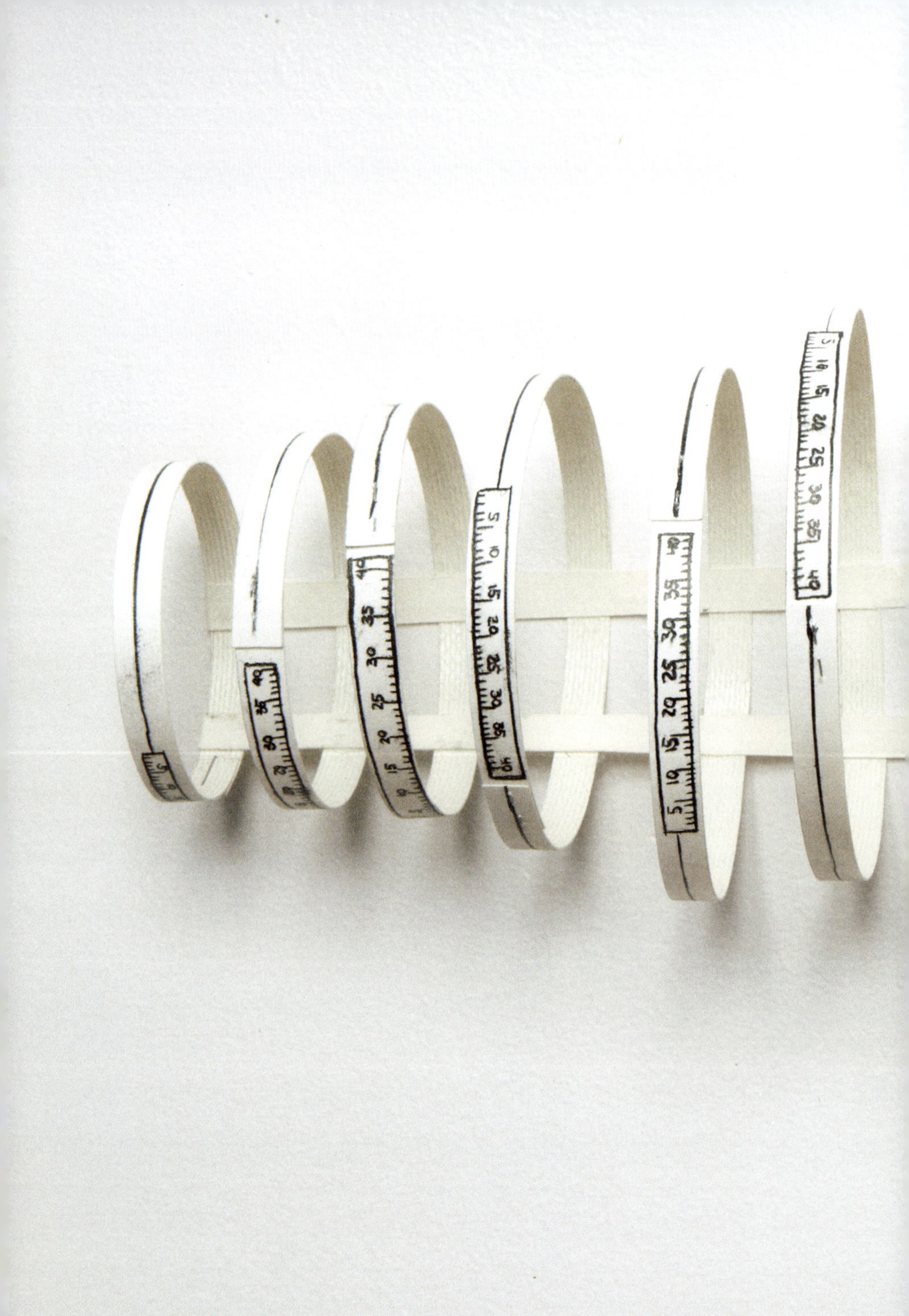

Untitled #3 (*Meta* series), 2010

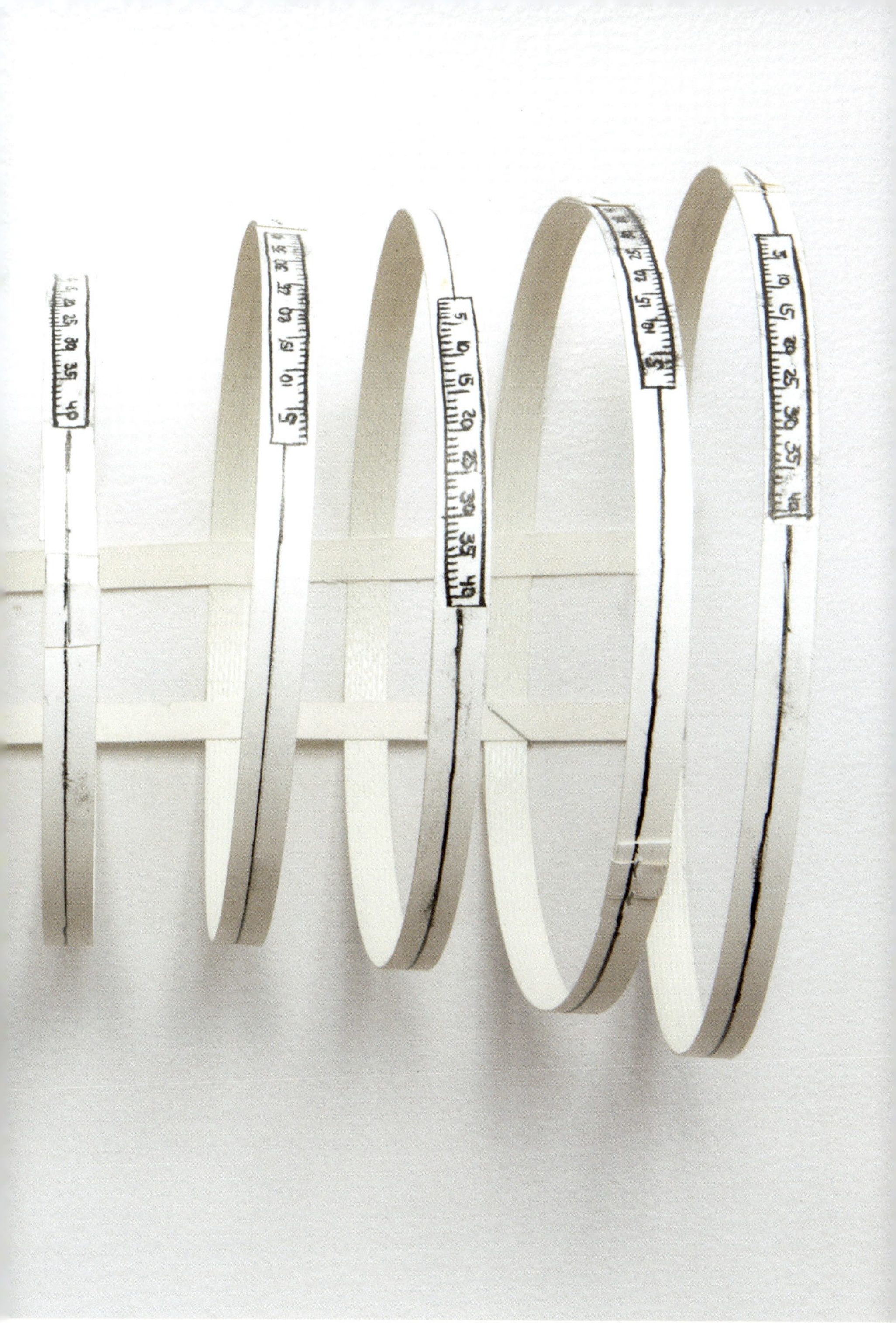

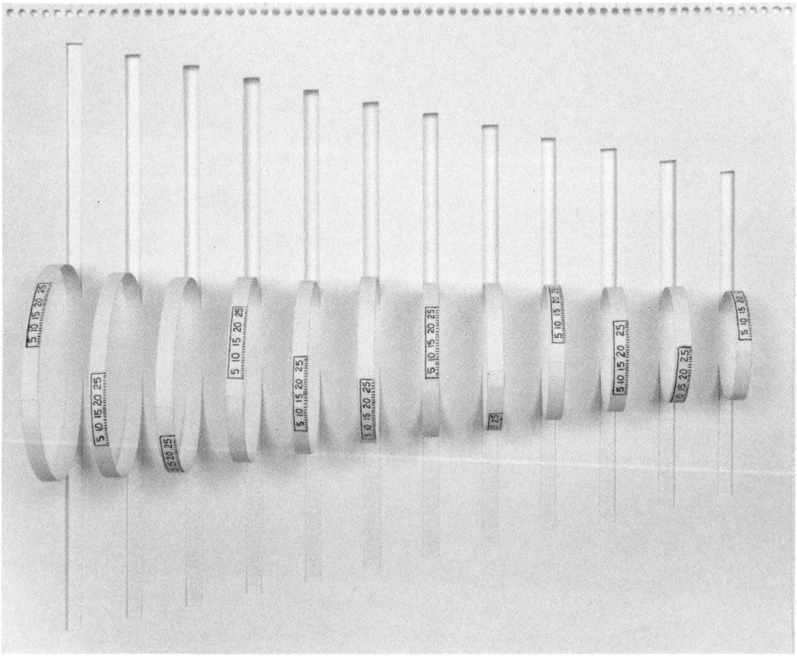

Untitled #2 (*Meta* series), 2010

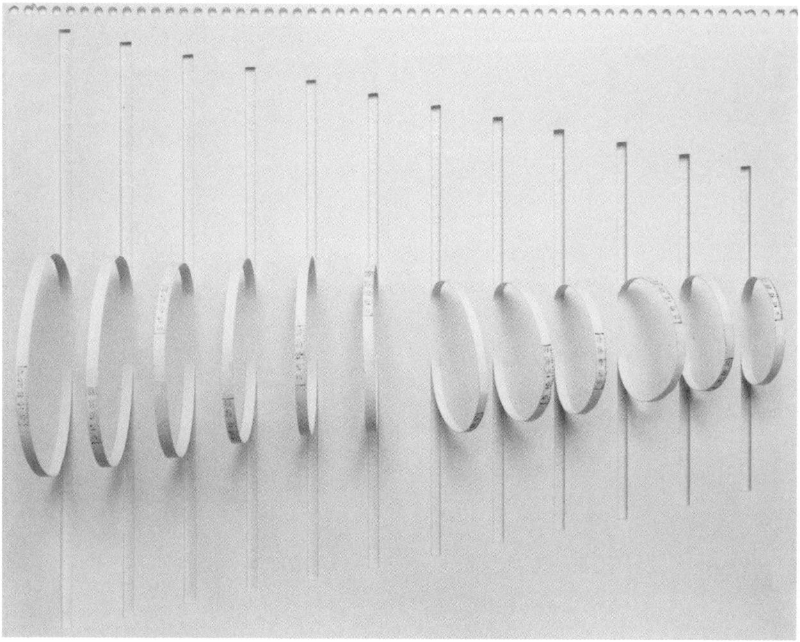

Untitled #4 (*Meta* series), 2010

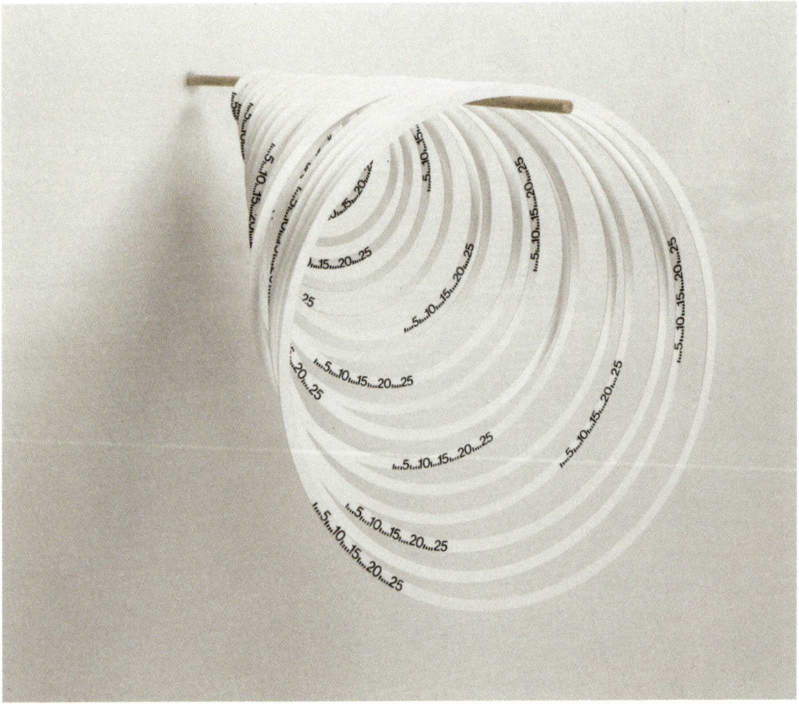

Untitled #6 (*Meta* series), 2010

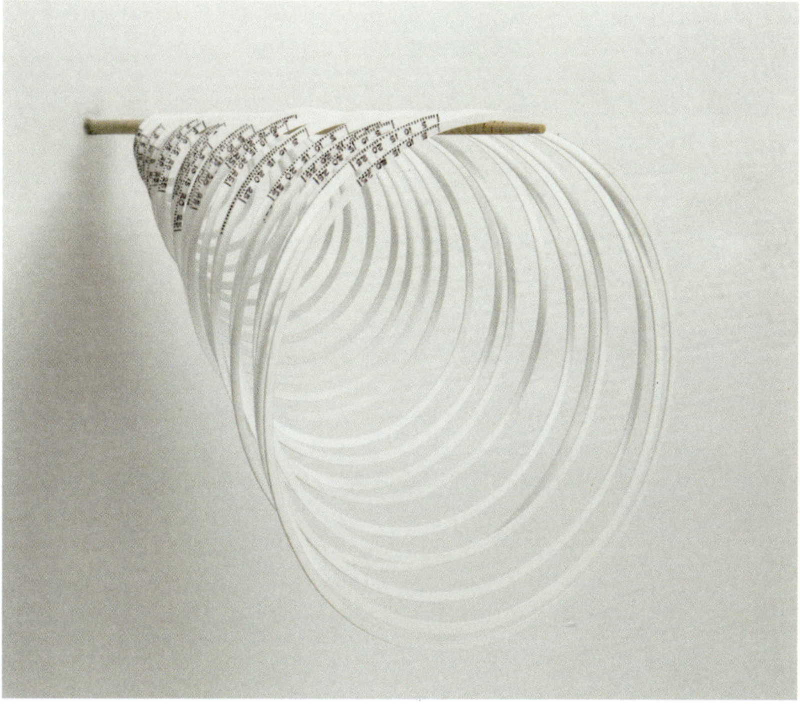

Untitled #7 (*Meta* series), 2010

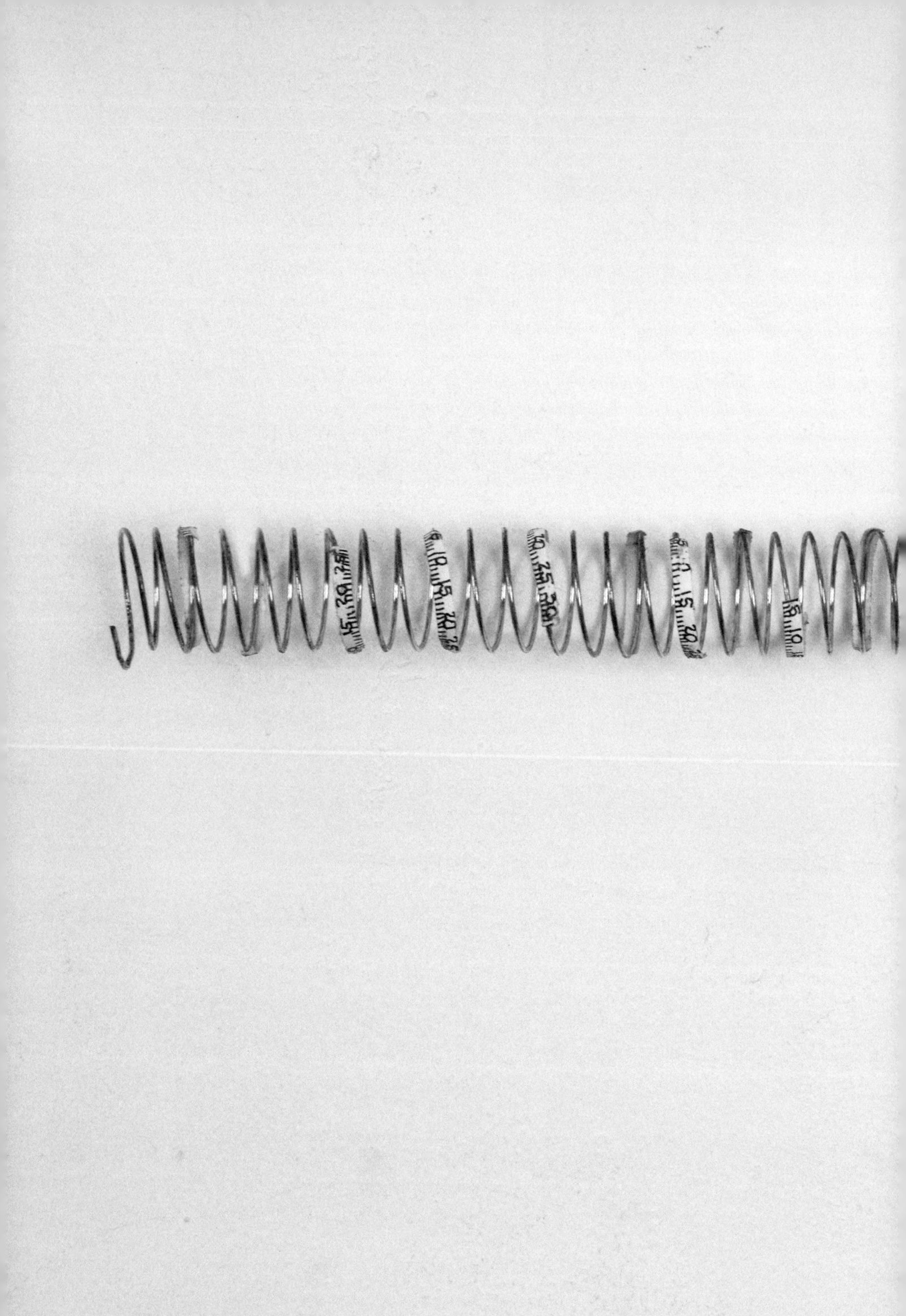

Untitled #8 (*Meta* series), 2010

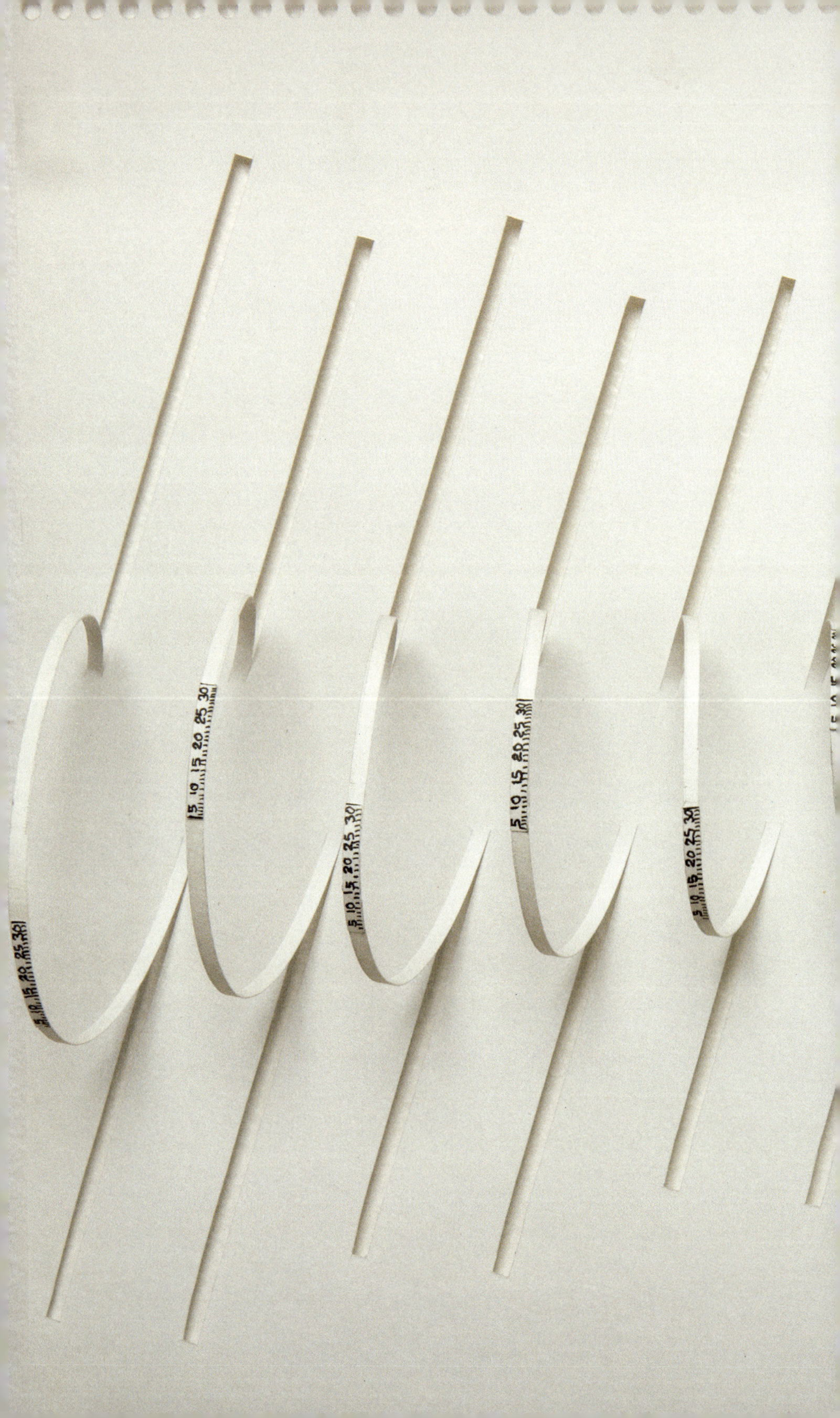
5 10 15 20 25 30
5 10 15 20 25 30
5 10 15 20 25 30
5 10 15 20 25 30
5 10 15 20 25 30

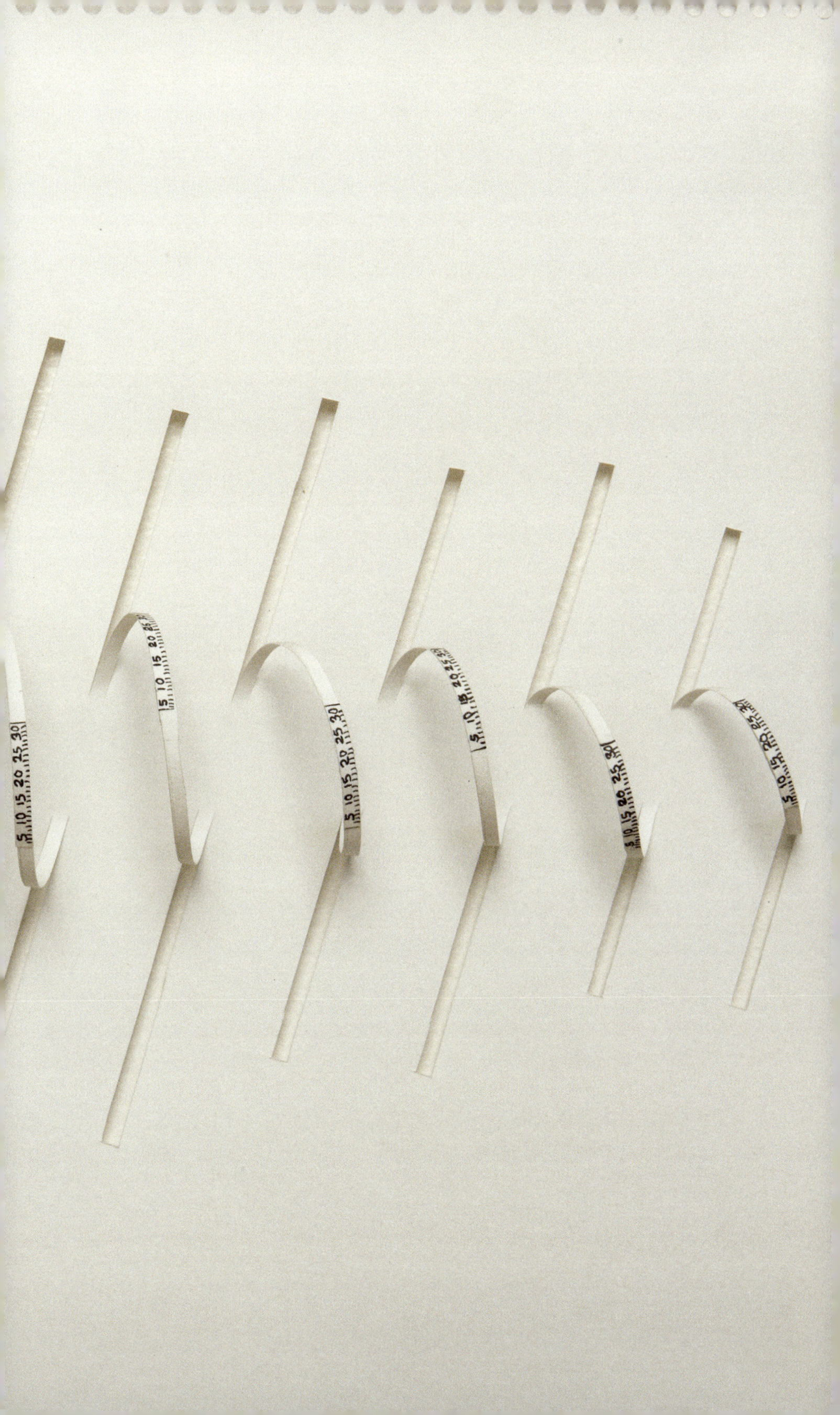

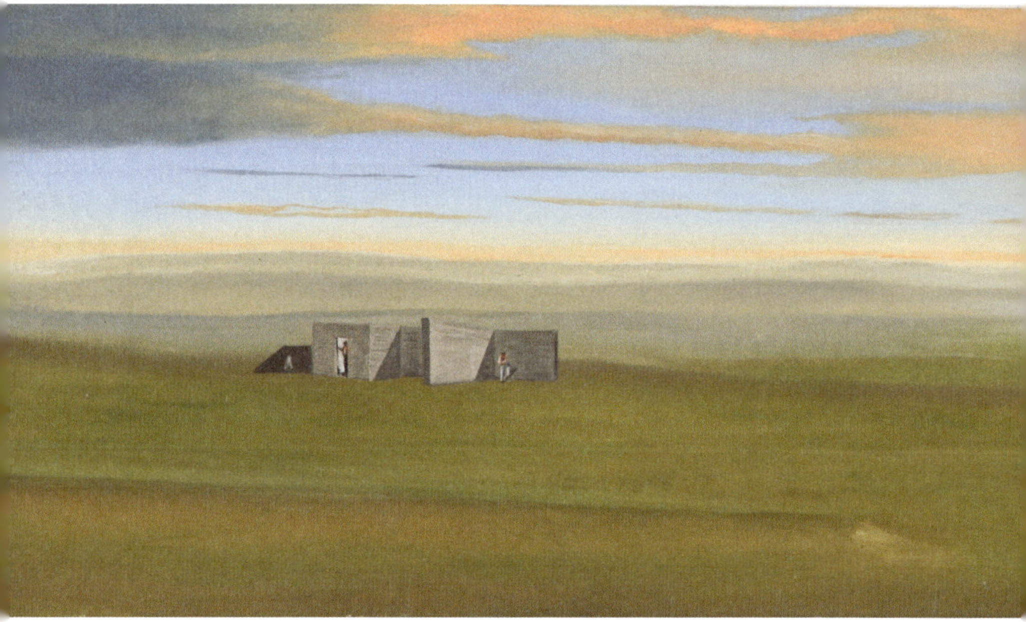

Preceding page: *Untitled #7* (*Meta* series), 2010
This page: *Ni me busques ... No me encuentras* (Don't Look For Me ... You Won't Find Me) [detail], 2003–2005

miguel angel ríos

by Raphael Rubinstein

Throughout his career, Miguel Angel Ríos has been engaged in a process of ceaseless artistic innovation across a range of mediums, from established modes such as collage, assemblage, drawing, and painting, to hybrid wall reliefs, multichannel videos, and sound works. The subjects of Ríos' art have been as varied as his materials and techniques, from pre-Columbian counting systems to contemporary conflicts in the Middle East, from children's games to hallucinogenic plants, from the colonization of the New World to 21st-century social struggles. The geography of his work—where it's made and the locations it evokes—has been equally expansive, stretching from New York City and Tepoztlán, Mexico, places where he maintains studios, to sites and regions throughout the Americas. Across the impressive range of Ríos' oeuvre, certain themes and structures recur. One of them is modularity, a compositional mode that appears in many of Ríos' works, from his pivotal *Gulf War* or *El Juego y el Dolor* series, 1991—dozens of mosaic like painted-cardboard assemblages made in response to the first Gulf War—to the recent trilogy of spinning-top videos *A Morir*, 2003, *On the Edge*, 2006, and *Aquí*, 2006. Modularity is also crucial to *Khipus* and *Maps*, the two series that first brought him wider attention in the mid-1990s.

Taking their name from the knotted cords that ancient Andean peoples employed as a counting system, the *Khipus* works translate statistical information about the past and present of Latin America into large-scale wall works made from knotted cords and pleated strips of canvas onto which the artist stenciled historical data.

Pleating is also central to the *Maps*, for which Ríos affixed reproductions of Colonial-era maps onto strips of canvas or cardboard that he then folded into accordion like shapes. In *Flor de la Civilización*, 1993, he transformed a Cibachrome photo of an early Spanish map of Mexico by slicing and pleating it into a series of concentric circles. Maps are often folded for convenience of storage and travel, but in Ríos' hands, folding becomes a critical act and a metaphor for the survival of indigenous traditions in postconquest Latin America. In both *Khipus* and *Maps*, Ríos seeks to reinvent ancient manual techniques while also assimilating the experiments of Post-Minimalism and Arte Povera.

If *Maps*, with its disrupting visual rhythms of pleated topography, exhibits modularity, it also announces a second of Ríos' preoccupations: landscape. Ríos began the *Maps* following extensive travels around South America, including the Calchaquies Valleys of northwestern Argentina where he was born, the forbidding Atacama Desert along the Chilean coast, and along the Amazon River. These voyages led Ríos to a deeper understanding of the monumentality of the South American landscape. For him, these "grand and infinite" spaces are "the landscape of terra incognita in relationship to Europe with its reduced and closed spaces."[1]

Ríos' art is often a response to the vast, sparsely populated, topologically dramatic landscapes of the Americas. For the artist, his intense involvement with monumentally scaled landscapes is one of the factors that distance him from the legacy of Joaquín Torres-García (1874–1949), the Uruguayan modernist who is often viewed as the father of Latin American art. Ríos insists that his "relation with South America comes from the other side," from "the destiny of having been born" in San Jose Norte Valles Calchaquies. He feels that Torres-García "never knew this landscape nor felt it; he is a European artist, with the concept of closed space inherited from Piet Mondrian." From this perspective, Ríos' work shares more with artists such as Jackson Pollock and Robert Smithson, who drew so deeply from open spaces of the North American continent.

While there is a certain anthropological aspect to Ríos' work, he has never followed the path of so many socially oriented conceptual artists who present their work as research or reportage. It's true that in preparing for a project, Ríos immerses himself in research and on-the-ground experience, but he is first and foremost a *creative* artist, someone who transforms whatever raw material he employs into an artwork that simultaneously transcends and celebrates its sources. His aim is not to express the identity of any particular culture; if he makes use of indigenous or popular Latin American material, it is only because it serves his deeper purpose—to create metaphors that illuminate universal human realities.

Still, it is hard to think of any other contemporary artist who has incorporated as broad a range of Latin American culture and history into his work.[2] Perhaps the best analogy for this aspect of Ríos' work is in the realm of music. In the early 1970s, fresh from composing the soundtrack for Bernardo Bertolucci's epochal *Last Tango in Paris*, Argentinean saxophonist Leandro "Gato" Barbieri embarked on a daring four-record exploration of Latin American music.[3] The recordings assembled a stellar lineup of musicians from throughout the Americas to perform compositions by Barbieri that drew on everything from Andean flute music to tango, bossa nova, samba, and big-band salsa. The distinctive granular wail of Barbieri's tenor saxophone threads through the diversity of styles and instruments, and song titles such as "Viva Emiliano Zapata" and "Para Nosotros" hint at the underlying political themes. Just as Barbieri fostered encounters between experimental jazz and indigenous Latin American musical styles, Ríos has joined the visual lexicon of Minimalism and Post-Minimalism with vernacular traditions of the Americas.

Like *El Juego y el Dolor*, the 2002 video *Ni me busques . . . No me encuentras* (Don't Look For Me. . . You Won't Find Me) marks a turning point in Ríos' career. It's the first fully realized work in the medium that has been Ríos' main focus during the last decade. Yet, *Ni me busques* is not only a video; it is also a series of paintings, drawings, and collages, all of which revolve around the same subject: a man wandering in a vast, arid landscape populated with apparitions. Ríos hasn't produced any paintings since *Ni me busques*, but all his subsequent videos have been accompanied by, and to a large degree grown out of, his drawings and collages. Even as his video productions have grown more elaborate, involving dozens of people, complex technology, and lengthy pre- and postproduction, Ríos has maintained his studio practice—the making of stuff by hand—as the driving force of his art.

The narrative of *Ni me busques* follows the artist—recognizable by his broad-brim hat—as he searches for peyote plants near the ghost town of Real de Catorce in the Mexican state of San Luis Potosí, which is situated on a high, dry plateau in the center of the country. The landscape in the video is dotted with mesquite and cacti, including the peyote cactus that figures prominently in the myths and rituals of the Huichol Indians. A single palm tree seems to be the only vegetation rising more than a few feet for many miles. Broad, low mountains are visible on the horizon; windswept clouds can be seen floating high above.

Everything in *Ni me busques* was filmed simultaneously by three adjacent cameras and is presented as a three-channel projection. The cameras mostly capture the same scenes from slightly different angles, but occasionally the footage is edited to be out of sync. As the video begins to convey the effects of ingesting peyote, the cameras start tilting unexpectedly, making the horizon seem like waves on a high sea and Ríos an unsteady ship upon it. The first of Ríos' hallucinations is presented with a striking matter-of-factness: Suddenly a seven-piece brass band, typical of small-town Mexican festivals, marches into view. Although nothing is more improbable than a brass band in the middle of a vast desert valley, Ríos, seemingly unsurprised, merely glances at the passing musicians and continues his altered-state walkabout.

Things rapidly get more intense as the artist flees an invisible train hurtling after him. The cameras, now obviously handheld, begin to wobble and tilt still more, at one point even turning upside down. The multiple, divergent views of the three-channel format correspond to certain effects of peyote, which have been eloquently described by the Belgian writer-artist Henri Michaux (1899–1984) in one of his books about his experiments with mescaline (which is derived from the peyote plant): "Multitude in your consciousness, a consciousness that expands to the point where it seems to double, to multiply, drunk with simultaneous perceptions and knowledge."[4] A dramatic doubling of consciousness occurs at the climax of the 10-minute video when Ríos enters a cinder-block structure that suddenly splits open with a crunching sound to reveal the artist doubled by his mirror image. As the twin figures merge, we see Ríos walk away into the Mexican desert.

Ni me busques ... No me encuentras is one of Ríos' most personal works. The culminating scene where he encounters the isolated house is a restaging of a recurring feature of his peyote trips. Repeatedly he would approach an adobe house that had magically appeared in the middle of the desert, but each time he tried to enter it, the building would split in two. As it split, Ríos would hear a sound that resembled the crust of a loaf of French bread being broken. Sometimes the adobe house was white and would divide into four parts, four separate planes. It was only later, in the wake of some flashbacks to his peyote experiences, that Ríos thought he understood the source of his hallucination. "It was the adobe house where I was born and that I later abandoned when I was 16 or 17 with the dream of traveling around the world. The sound, the sound of the bread breaking, is the warm bread that my mother used to make and then bake behind the house." Ríos believes that it is an abiding sense of guilt for having run away from his hometown, which he recalls as "so beautiful" (*tan hermoso*), that triggered the peyote hallucination—and the video, paintings, and drawings it inspired.

As in most of Ríos' subsequent videos, the making of *Ni me busques* involved months of planning, numerous technical challenges, and lots of on-the-spot improvisation. Today, Ríos recalls it as a "crazy adventure" that he and cinematographer Rafael Ortega undertook. Chief among the difficulties of filming was the extreme heat of the desert and omnipresent cactus spines. Peyote, of course, was the key component of the experience. Under its influence, Ríos felt an incredible energy that sustained him during the arduous 10-day shoot. At a certain point, Ortega also began to ingest small amounts of peyote because there was no other way to keep up with Ríos' creative velocity. Ríos and his small crew also realized that peyote helped them tolerate the desert heat, something the Huichol had discovered centuries before. A crucial point came early on after some initial footage had been shot with a single video camera. Ríos wasn't satisfied with the results because they didn't convey the spatial monumentality of the landscape. The solution was to mount three Sony video cameras side by side on a steel harness (made by a local welder) that Ortega could wear on his chest. For some shots, however, Ríos turned to other options: once handing the cameras to the crew's driver, Luis Munguia, who had never operated a video camera in his life; on another occasion bringing equipment all the way from Mexico City for a dolly shot.

For all its personal associations, *Ni me busques* resonates with Mexican art history. One can't help noticing that the split and doubled cinder-block building resembles an Olmec stone mask. It's also clear, as the artist confirms, that his cinematographic vision of curving horizons and distant mountains is indebted to the panoramic landscapes of Dr. Atl (1875–1964), Mexico's greatest 20th-century landscape painter, whose aerial views of his nation's valleys and volcanoes frequently showed the curvature of the earth. Less obviously, the three-channel projection subtly imitates the tripartite design of traditional Catholic altarpieces. Interestingly, the adjacent images in Ni me busques and Ríos' other multichannel projections constitute a kind of folded/hinged structure that connects them to Ríos' *Khipus* and *Maps* works of the 1990s.

The paintings, drawings, and collages that accompany *Ni me busques* are also rich in art-historical echoes that reach beyond Mexico. Thanks to their stark shadows and artificial emptiness, many of them evoke Giorgio de Chirico's metaphysical landscapes, while others suggest René Magritte, both in their surreal subject matter and uninflected paint handling. (At times, Ríos' self-portrayals suggest a Latin American version of Magritte's bowler-hatted Everyman.) More contemporary connections are made with the images of open boxes, roofless houses, and freestanding walls that Ríos playfully manipulates in the paintings. As well as serving as disorienting settings for the peyote-trip scenarios, these eccentric geometric structures obliquely resemble two landmarks of the postwar Brazilian avant-garde: Lygia Clark's *Bichos* and Helio Oiticica's *Bólides*. Like Oiticica (whose New York studio Rios visited in the 1970s) and Clark, Ríos understands geometry as an adjunct to the human body, and not as a separate realm of autonomous forms.

The title *Ni me busques … No me encuentras* sounds like a riddle: "Don't look for me. You won't find me. What am I?" It could be the peyote plant speaking. By opening up his art to the visionary revelations of natural psychedelics, Ríos is aligning himself with predecessors such as Michaux, who made many drawings under the influence of mescaline, and German artist Sigmar Polke (1941–2010), who frequently celebrated the psychic power of magic mushrooms in his work. Ultimately, however, drugs are not central to this artist: None of his subsequent work has derived from, nor even alluded to, psychedelic experiences. Nor, as we have seen, is he simply concerned with anthologizing Latin American culture, even through *Ni me busques*. In fact, peyote may not even be the main subject of the multimedium ensemble that constitutes *Ni me busques*, which seems rather to be an extended meditation on artistic inspiration. Like the peyote plant, the germ of a new work sometimes doesn't want to be found, but it's always ready, if treated with respect, to deliver unforeseen—and sometimes unsettling—revelations. Looking at the impressive sequence of works from *Khipus* and *Maps* to *Ni me busques. . .No me encuentras* to 2010's *Mecha* (Fuse), it's clear that Miguel Angel Ríos has gained access to just such revelations over and over again—and so have we, his viewers.

1 E-mail to the author, August 23, 2011. All subsequent quotes from Miguel Angel Ríos are from e-mails to the author on August 23–28, 2011, and a telephone conversation on August 28, 2011. I have translated certain passages from the e-mails from Spanish into English.

2 The trilogy of spinning-top videos is inspired by *trompos*, a game played throughout Latin America. Similarly, *Mecha*, 2010, began with another popular pastime, the Colombian game of *tejo*, which is based on a pre-Columbian sport. In the dramatic videos *Crudo* and *White Suit*, both 2008, and *Matambre*, 2009, featuring performances by a dancer and a pack of vicious dogs, Ríos draws on the culture of his native Argentina (gaucho dances and the sport of *boleadoras*), as well as Spanish flamenco, North American tap dance, and dance styles from Veracruz, Mexico.

3 The recordings are *Chapter One: Latin America*, 1973, *Chapter Two: Hasta Siempre*, 1973, *Chapter Three: Viva Emiliano Zapata*, 1974, and *Chapter Four: Alive in New York*, 1975. For

listeners who only know of Barbieri as a purveyor of Latin-tinged smooth jazz, these earlier experiments may come as a surprise.

4 Henri Michaux, *Knowledge Through the Abyss*, 1961, in *Darkness Moves: An Henri Michaux Anthology*, ed. and trans. David Ball, Berkeley, University of California Press, 1994, p. 212. Another intriguing parallel between Michaux and Ríos is their emphasis on the fold as process and metaphor. Michaux celebrates folding in his 1949 collection of poems *La Vie Dans les Plis* (Life in the Folds).

Raphael Rubinstein is a New York-based poet and art critic whose numerous books include *Polychrome Profusion: Selected Art Criticism 1990–2002* (Hard Press Editions) and *The Afterglow of Minor Pop Masterpieces* (Make Now). From 1997 to 2007 he was a senior editor at *Art in America*, where he continues to be a contributing editor. He is currently professor of critical studies at the University of Houston and is also on the faculty of the Art Criticism and Writing MFA Program at the School of Visual Arts in New York. In 2002, the French government presented him with the award of Chevalier in the Order of Arts and Letters.

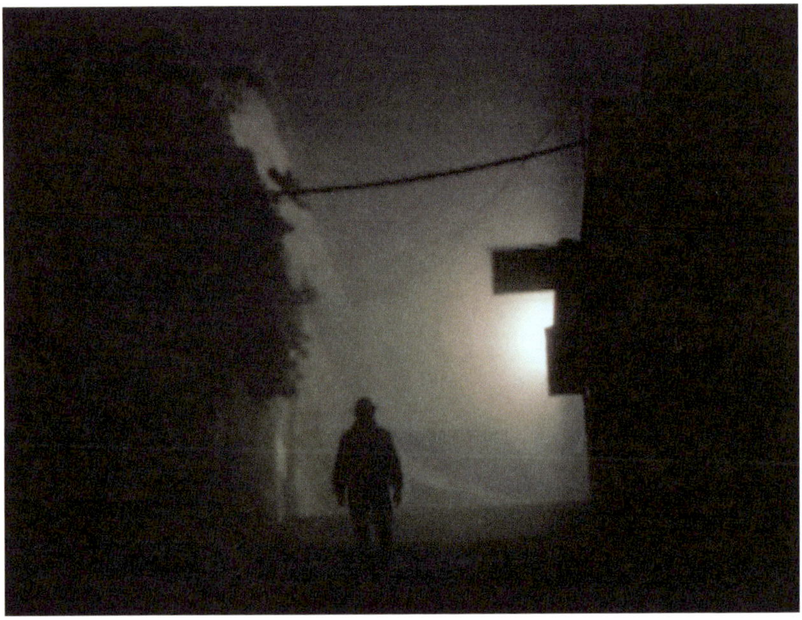

Los niños brotan de noche (The Children Spring Forth from the Night), 2002 (video still)

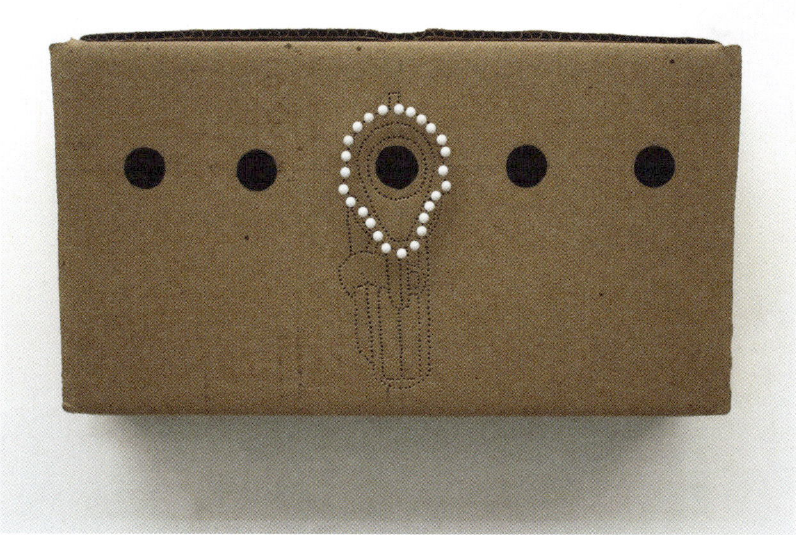

SendEx Box # 1, 2011

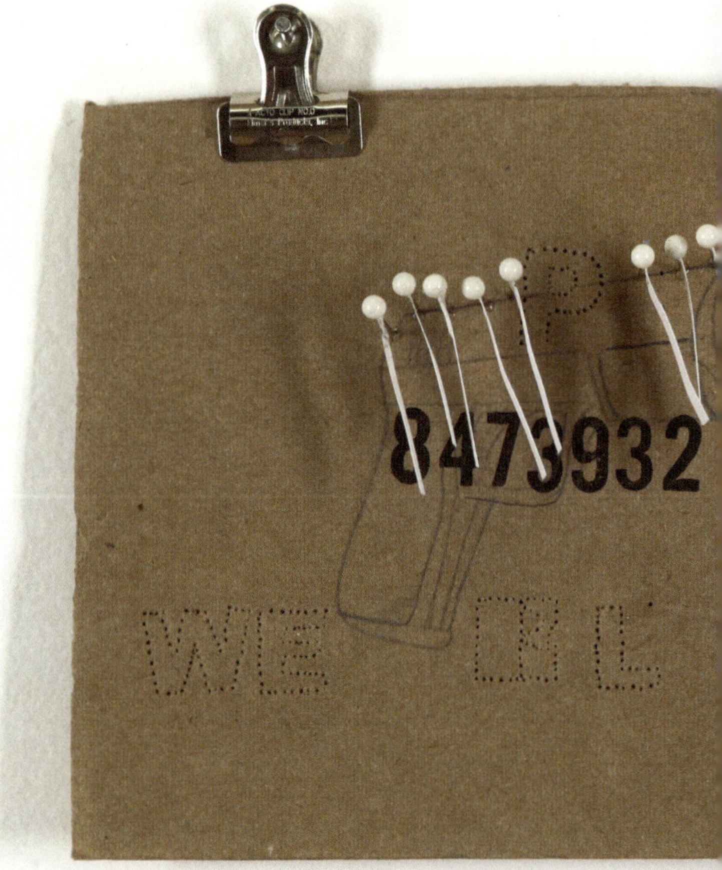

Untitled, 2011

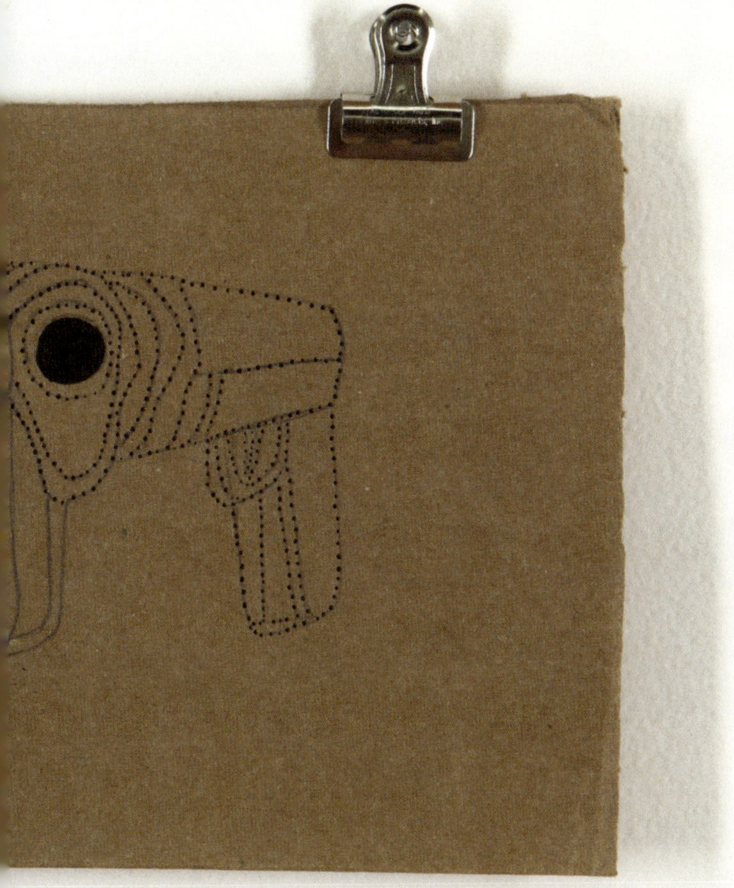

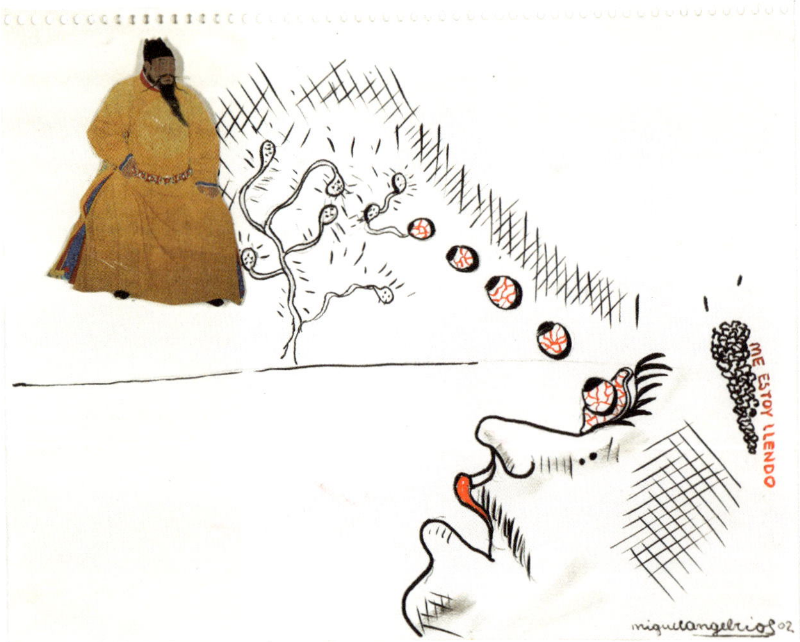

Hallucinogenic Trip #47 from *El viaje del botanista* (The Botanist's Journey), 1997–2002

the botanist's journey

by Julieta González

In general, we experience life from a rather limited point of view. This is the so-called normal state. However, through hallucinogens, the perception of reality can be strongly changed and expanded. These different aspects or levels of one and the same reality are not mutually exclusive. They form an all-encompassing, timeless, transcendental reality.

Richard Evans Schultes and Albert Hofmann. *Plants of the Gods: Their Sacred, Healing, and Hallucinogenic Powers.*[1]

For the past three decades, Miguel Angel Ríos has engaged in a poetic, and at times unwittingly critical, dissection of the discourses that have projected art from Latin America into the international arena—from identity politics to a particular brand of Latin American postcolonialism. The indigenous past of the Americas and its incidence on the continents' contemporary cultures is a recurring theme in his work. In earlier works based on ancient cartographies of the New World, Ríos dismantled the rationale of the map, reconfiguring it into a dysfunctional model based on displacements and contingencies. This interest in ordering structures led him to work with other systems of representation, such as botanical illustration and the field methods of the naturalist and the ethnographer.

In the late 1990s, and after traveling to regions as diverse as the Amazon Basin and the Chihuahuan Desert, Ríos began to develop a body of work through which he addressed the meaning of hallucinogenic plants in the indigenous cultures of the American continents—a new cartography of the Americas but this time through other means of representation that account for the artist's subjective voyage into the territories of alterity.

To understand Ríos' undertaking in this body of work, it is necessary to contextualize it in terms of the tradition of ethnographic and botanical pursuits in the Americas during the Colonial period. The visualization of virgin territory by explorers during this period has been categorized by Mary Louise Pratt and Craig Owens[2] as fundamentally one of prospection, and it served very precise political and economic purposes: It was aimed at facilitating the process of colonization and exploitation of the land. These landscapes were viewed as prospects—resources to be exploited, land to be cultivated and occupied. In this sense, botany and cartography were instrumental to this task of prospection and evaluation of territory. In his earlier work, Ríos dismantled the cartographic enterprise of colonial interests in the Americas. The same spirit animates his dissection of botany and ethnography in these works, which attempt to identify cultural forms erased during the process of colonization. The specific use of diverse media such as drawing, photography, and video, and their incidence in the final presentation of the work in the exhibition space, raises questions about the authority of ethnographic observation and its claims to objectivity based on the indexical capabilities of its documentary apparatus—one that has been instrumental in the construction of an iconography of otherness.

While we could not affirm that Ríos engages in a systematic interpellation of ethnographic observation and representation—at least not in the same way that artists and filmmakers such as Juan Downey, Lothar Baumgarten, or Jean Rouch have in their respective practices—his approach is quite singular in its genre and offers yet another insight on a subject that has been a central concern for contemporary anthropology. Ríos addresses the subject of alterity from an "altered state," destabilizing the position of the observer by producing the majority of these works under the influence of the different alkaloids derived from these plants: toloache (*Datura inoxia*), teonanácatl (*Psilocybe mexicana*), and peyote (*Lophophora williamsii*).

Under different states of altered consciousness, the artist attempts to record the hallucinogenic experience of each of these plants in their local context and with the aid of shamans and other spiritual guides.

Ríos chose to use specific mediums for the documentation of each experience. A series of drawings made under the influence of the peyote cactus conveys in the manner of automatic writing the delirium of the artist under the effects of the drug, but more importantly the drawings signal the impossibility of representing the hallucinogenic experience and the twofold nature of drawing: While no longer serving the purpose of documentation, it brings out the subjective nature of the experience and underscores our presence as mere outside spectators who cannot wholly grasp its intensity and significance.

In the series of photographs depicting the toloache flowers, Ríos specifically addresses the purported objectivity of the photographic document. Photography was instrumental in the development of ethnographic practice, as its portrayal of reality conferred authenticity to fieldwork observations. The whimsical and highly stylized paintings and drawings of traveling artists who often accompanied explorers and prospectors to the Americas in the 17th, 18th, and 19th centuries hardly conformed to the analytical and detail-oriented standards of the nascent field of anthropology. Ríos undermines the indexicality of the photograph, because even though the device remains the same, it becomes an instrument for Ríos to register his own subjective experience, whereby he becomes the subject of his own research. The camera thus does not afford us a view of these plants or their use in these indigenous cultures, but rather becomes an instrument of introspection and is placed at the service of the artist's distorted perception. Moreover, Ríos further contaminates the use of the photographic medium by placing the color dots that characterized his earlier maps within the frame of the picture, coexisting with the flowers and people—including himself-portrayed in the photographs.

Two other pieces pertaining to this body of work challenge the function of the document in the act of representation.

The installation *Toloache: Mapping with the Mind*, 2000-2001, of which different iterations have been exhibited since its first presentation at the 2000 Havana Biennale,[3] mainly features a completely darkened interior where the floor has been padded with foam panels of different thicknesses, in turn covered by a carpet. Within this room, spectators can listen to a sound recording of the artist's experience with hallucinogenic mushrooms guided by a female shaman (Doña Gudelia). In this space, the spectator loses all sense of place and orientation; it is impossible to know in the pitch-black darkness where the space ends and if it is a large or a small room. The irregular floor makes spectators lose their footing, further intensifying initial loss of spatial coordinates. The sound recording is an uncanny succession of chants, wails, and exclamations by the artist, the shaman, and other people involved in the session. In terms of documenting the experience, the recording scarcely sheds light on the particulars of this type of shamanic ritual, much less about the experience itself. As with most of the works in this series, it points toward the impossibility of representing such experiences. However, the different sensations experienced within that darkened space can be likened to those felt during drug-induced delirium: loss of the notions of limit and place, loss of referent, loss of the notion of the real, loss of equilibrium. We lose ourselves as subjects in that darkened room. We also lose ourselves as observers and spectators, and we enter a space of indetermination, a void from which the artist offers us the possibility to challenge univocal constructions of culture. Furthermore, this work introduces the problem of enunciation, the fragile platform from which the observational discourse is articulated, and the correlation that exists between the solidity of that platform and the legitimacy of the discourse.

Los niños brotan de noche (The Children Spring Forth from the Night), in allusion to the fact that the Mazatec people give the name of "children" to the psilocybe mushrooms, is a video in which Ríos once again documents an experience with hallucinogenic mushrooms. Contrary to the sound installation—where the spectator is significantly involved—this video addresses the problem of documentation and the role it plays in lending credence to ethnographic representation. This video was made by Ríos with the aid of a camera operator and a sound technician, who also took the alkaloid. As a result, the video image is blurry and dark, and we can hardly see the action that takes place during the ceremonial taking of the mushrooms. However, this absence of a clear image reveals the artist's intention of sub-utilizing the medium, and thus of producing an inconclusive document. Under the influence of these alkaloids, vision and sound are distorted, and it is impossible to convey a clear image. In the audio installation, we cannot completely grasp what is happening or understand what is being said; the same goes for the photographs and the video.

What is notable about Ríos' *sui generis* approach is the close correlation between the mediums and exhibition strategies that he employs and the specific questions he raises in regard to Western culture's construction of alterity, with his particular deconstruction of ethnographic and representational canons through his exploration of the use of hallucinogenic plants in prehispanic cultures. From the subjective experience of altered consciousness, the artist reconstructs an image of the other that is indistinct and indeterminate. In the process, he destabilizes the rationality of Western systems of representation and challenges the cultural authority of the modern Western world and its canonical definitions of otherness.

1 McGraw-Hill, New York, 1979.

2 In his discussion of the work of Lothar Baumgarten in the essay "Improper Names," Craig Owens quotes Mary Louise Pratt's argument on prospection and explains how Baumgarten's black-and-white photographs of the Gran Sabana "explicitly refer to the interest that transforms the landscape into a prospect and the viewer into a prospector." Craig Owens, "Improper Names" from *Beyond Recognition: Representation, Power, and Culture* (University of California Press, 1994). Mary Louise Pratt, "Scratches on the Face of the Country; Or, What Mr. Barrow Saw in the Land of The Bushmen," from *Critical Inquiry* (Fall 1985).

3 Though the work consists of a wooden hut with a darkened interior in which a sound recording is continuously playing, Ríos presented this work in the exhibition *El Viaje del Botanista*, November 2001–January 2002, which I curated at the Sala Mendoza in Caracas, Venezuela, as a room integrated into the architecture of the exhibition space, not as a separate structure, so that it was impossible to distinguish its dimensions from the outside, thus heightening the disorientating effect. It is to this precise installation that I refer in this essay.

Julieta González is associate curator of Latin American Art at Tate Modern, London and an independent curator. From 1997–1998 she was a Helena Rubinstein Curatorial Fellow at the Whitney Independent Study Program, and curator of contemporary art at the Museo Alejandro Otero and Museo de Bellas Artes de Caracas from 1999–2003. In 2009 she co-curated the *2nd Trienal Poligráfica de San Juan, Latinoamérica y el Caribe* along with Adriano Pedrosa and Jens Hoffmann. She has edited several artist books and written essays for international publications and catalogs.

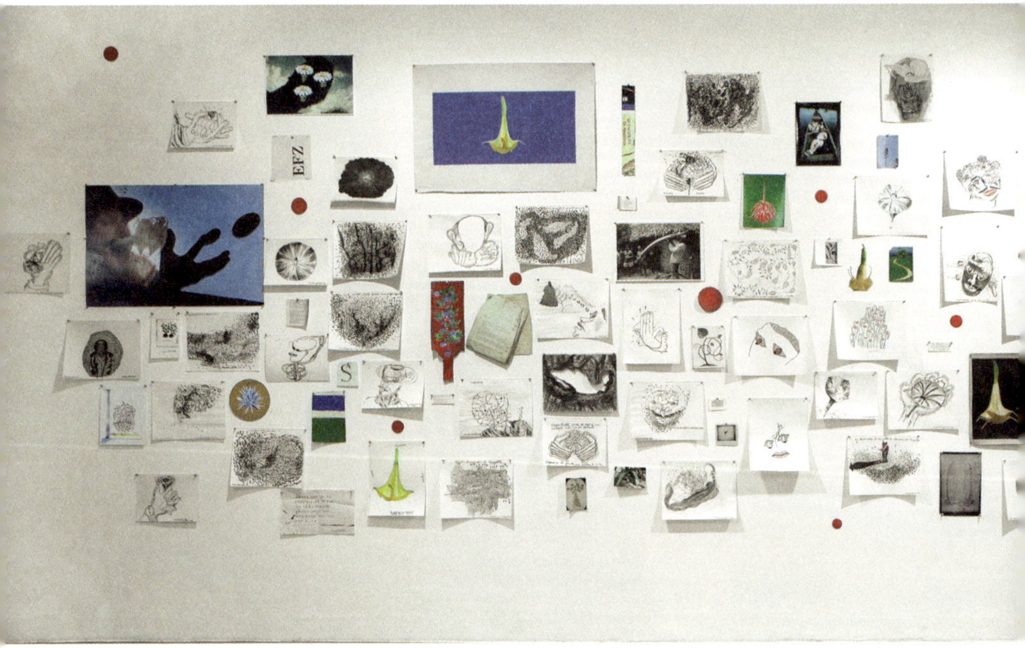

El viaje del botanista (The Botanist's Journey), 1997–2002

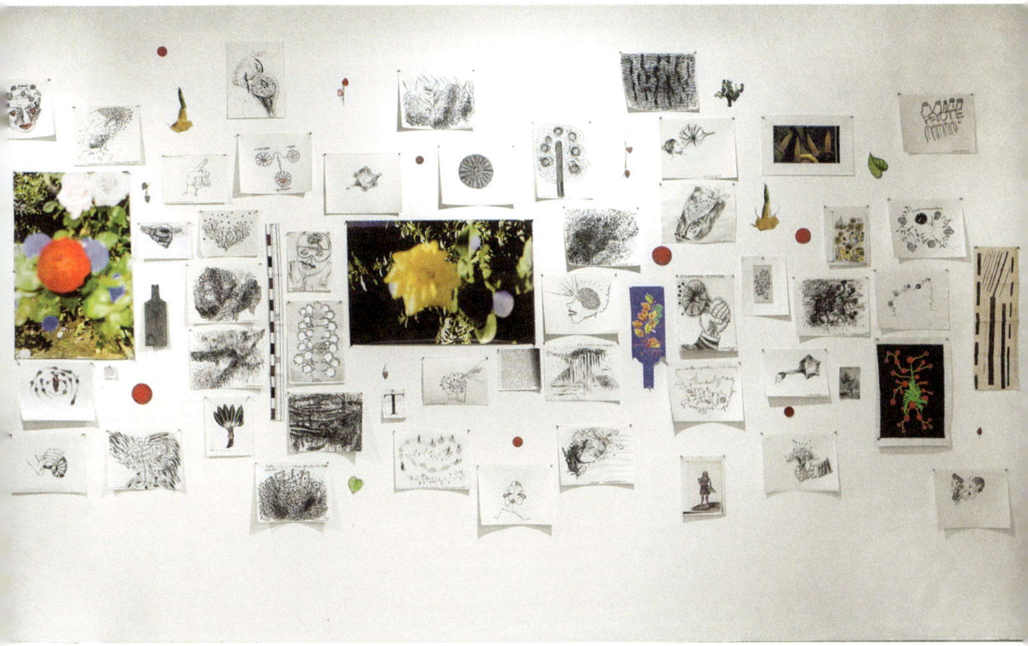

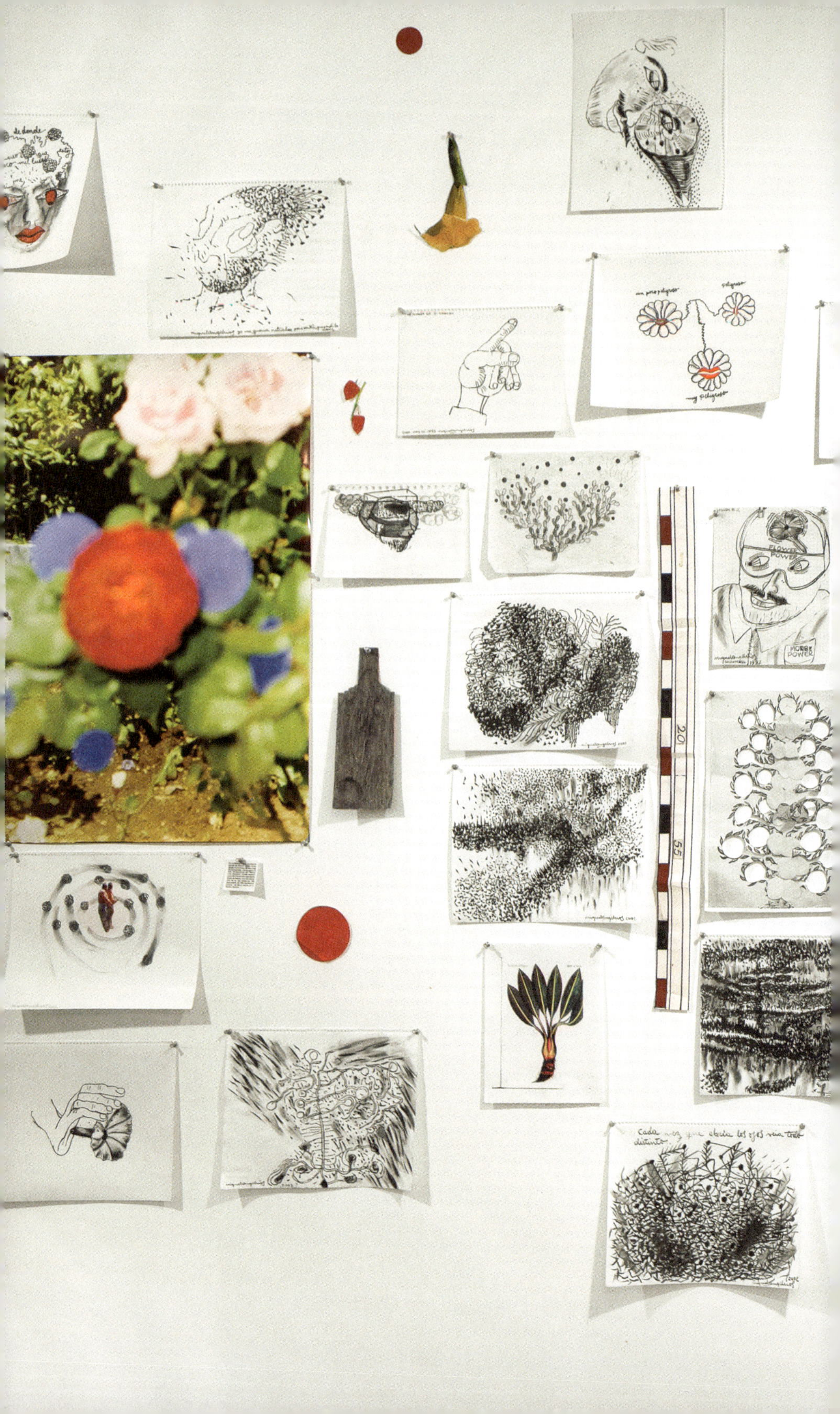

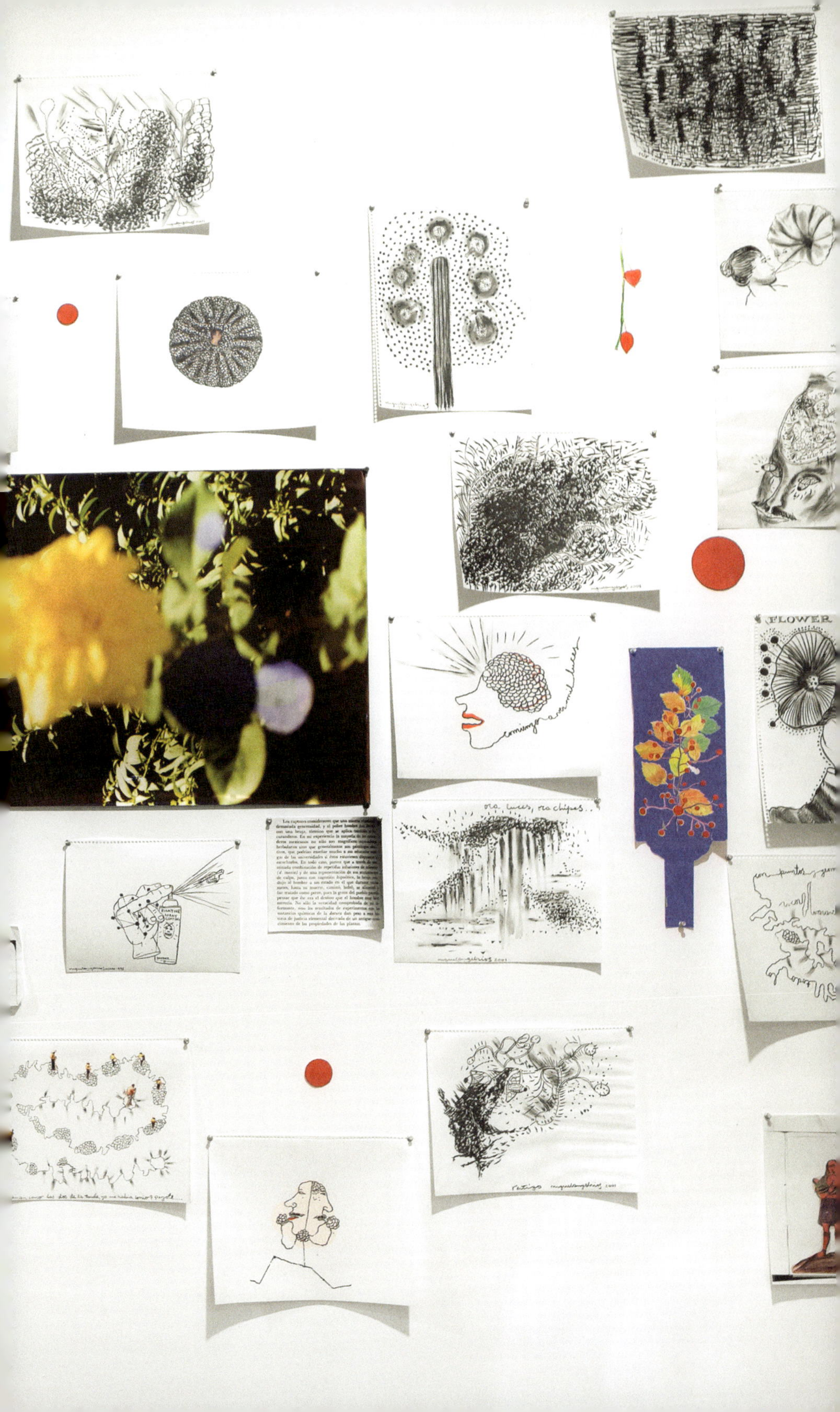
FLOWER

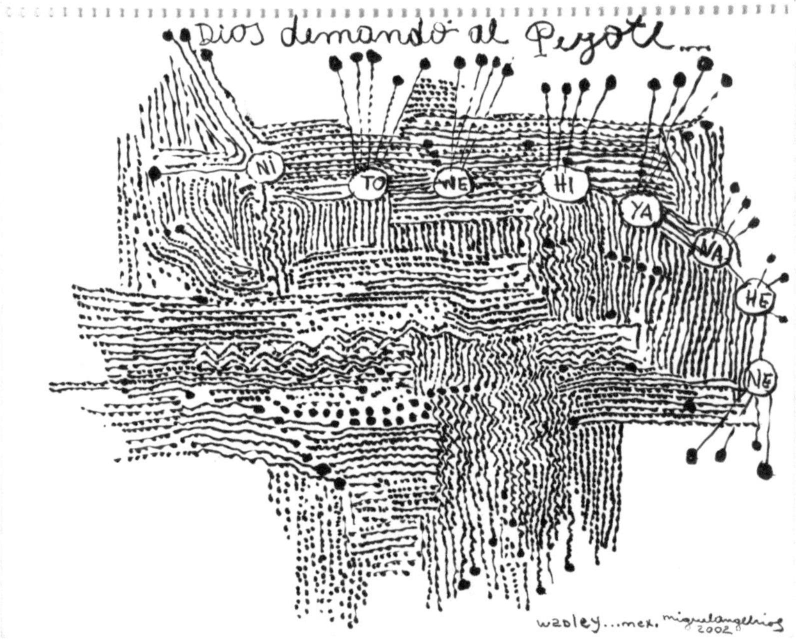

Preceding page: *El viaje del botanista* (The Botanist's Journey), 1997–2002
This page: *Hallucinogenic Trip #1* from *El viaje del botanista* (The Botanist's Journey), 1997–2002

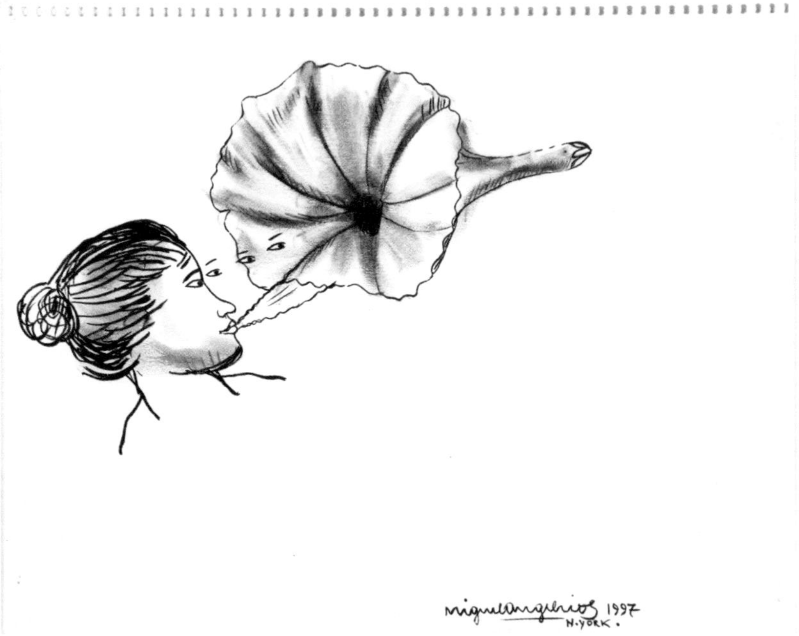

Hallucinogenic Trip #3 from *El viaje del botanista* (The Botanist's Journey), 1997–2002

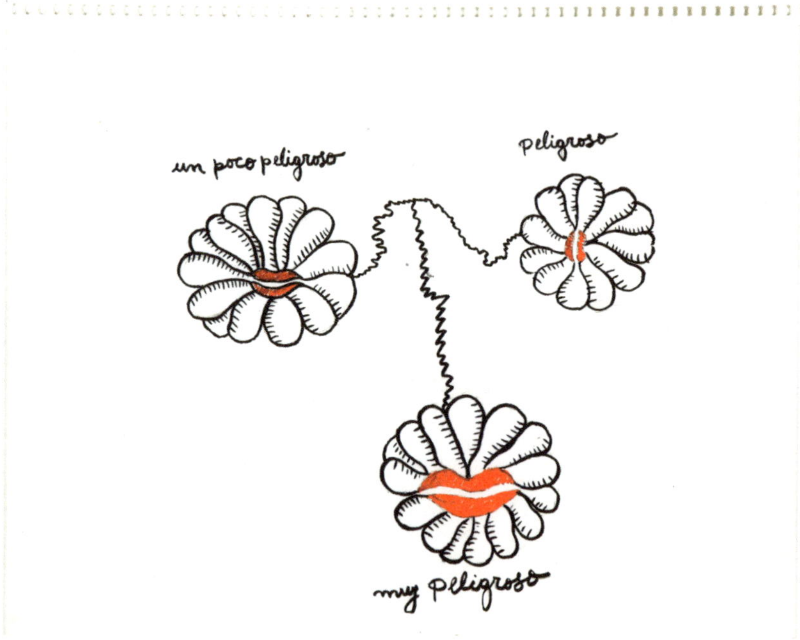

Hallucinogenic Trip #5 from *El viaje del botanista* (The Botanist's Journey), 1997–2002

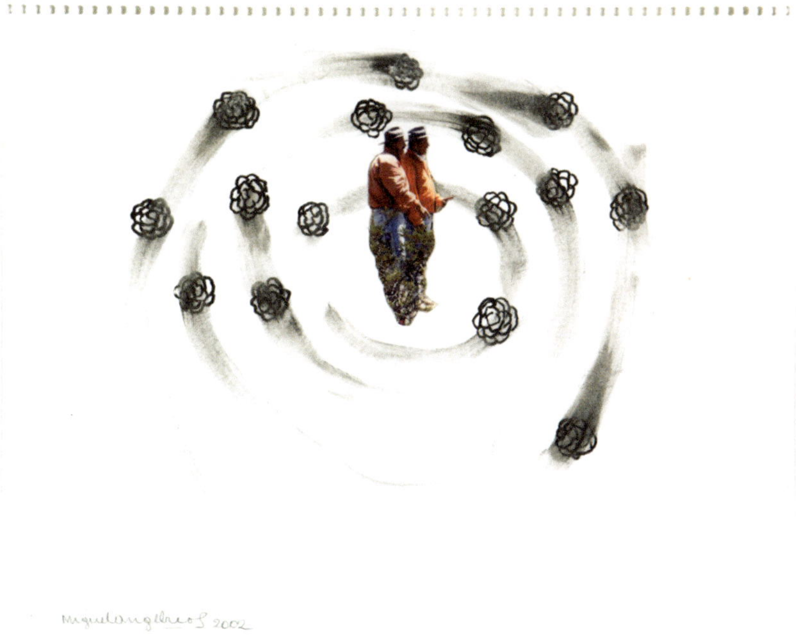

Hallucinogenic Trip #6 from *El viaje del botanista* (The Botanist's Journey), 1997–2002

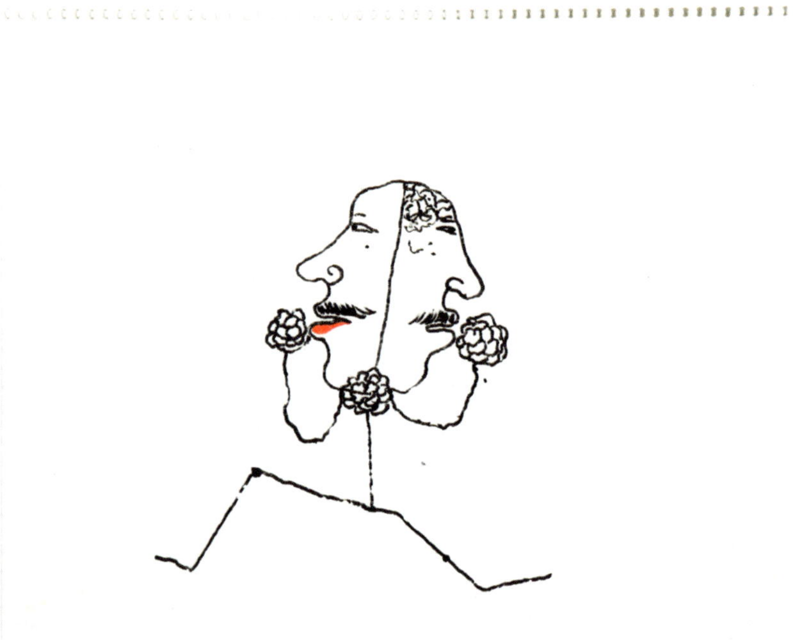

Hallucinogenic Trip #12 from *El viaje del botanista* (The Botanist's Journey), 1997–2002

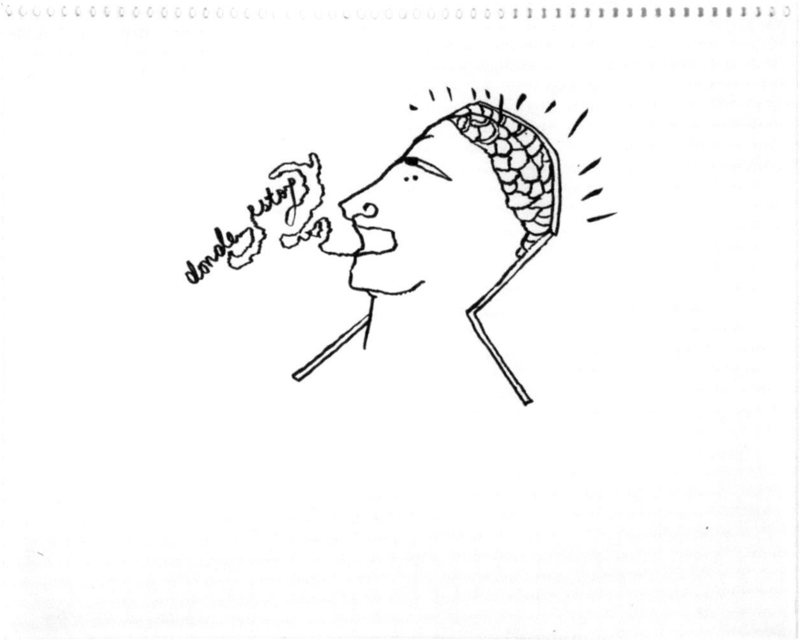

Hallucinogenic Trip #13 from *El viaje del botanista* (The Botanist's Journey), 1997–2002

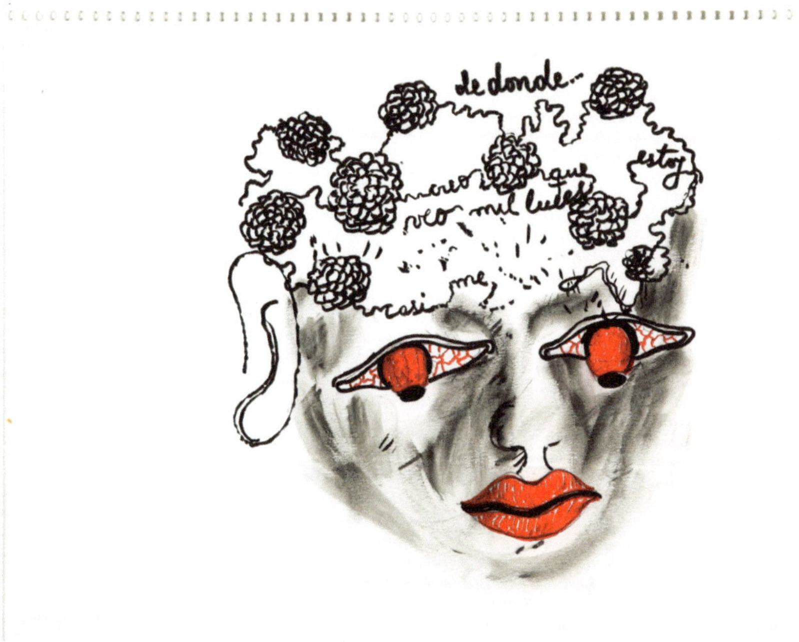

Hallucinogenic Trip #15 from *El viaje del botanista* (The Botanist's Journey), 1997–2002

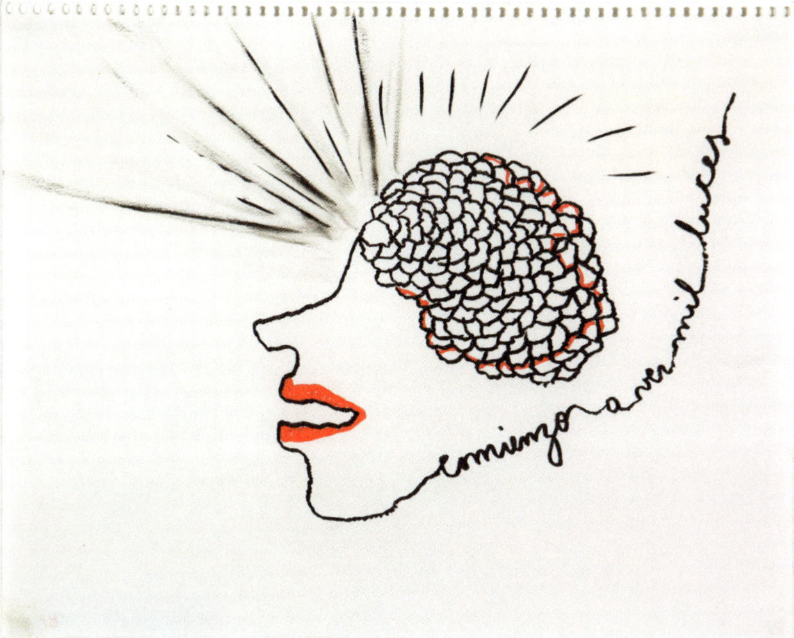

Hallucinogenic Trip #16 from *El viaje del botanista* (The Botanist's Journey), 1997–2002

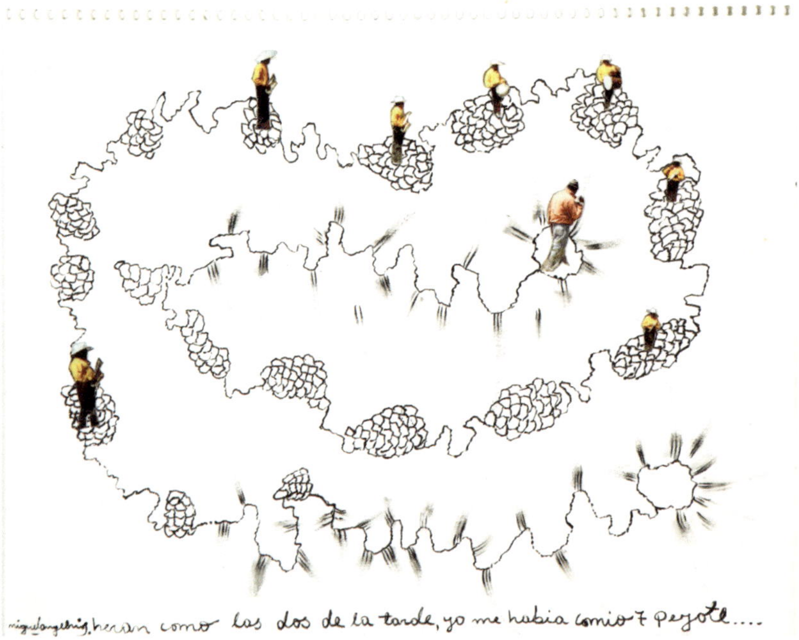

Hallucinogenic Trip #17 from *El viaje del botanista* (The Botanist's Journey), 1997–2002

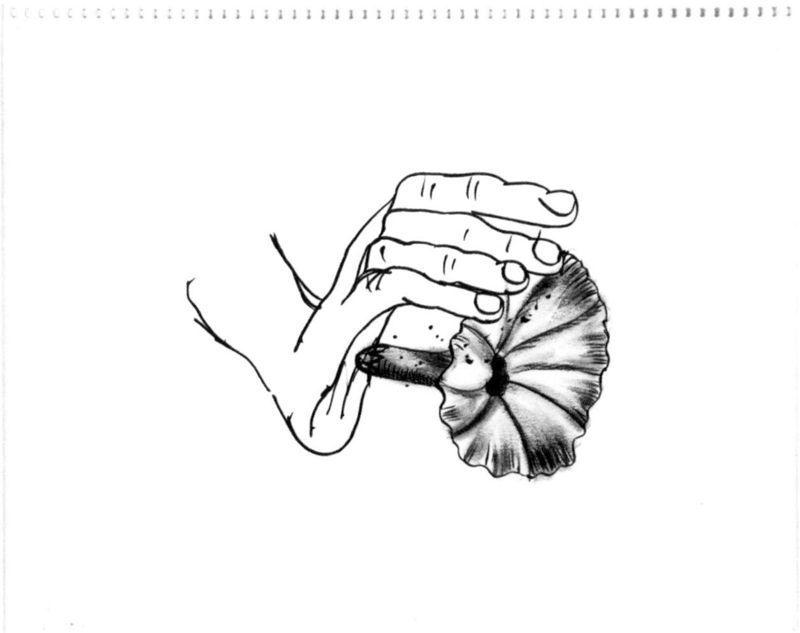

Hallucinogenic Trip from *El viaje del botanista* (The Botanist's Journey), 1997–2002

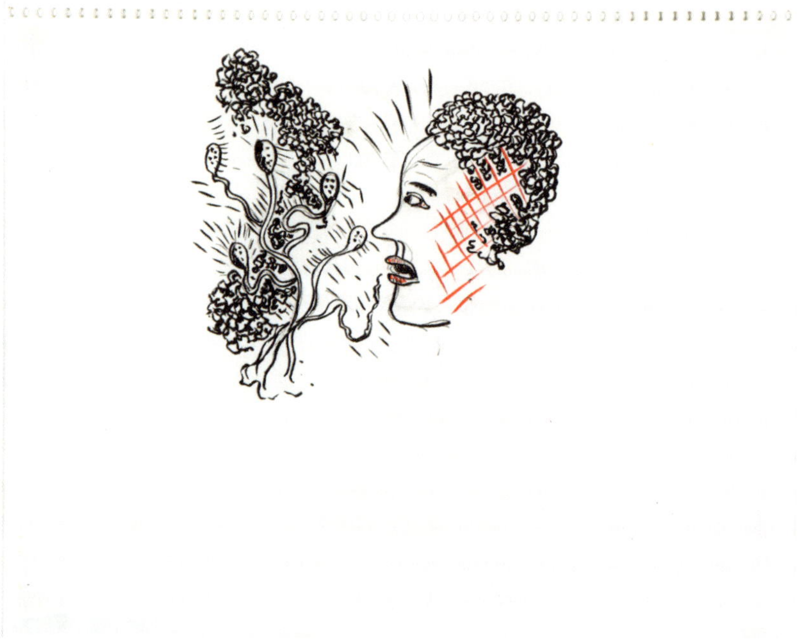

Hallucinogenic Trip #19 from *El viaje del botanista* (The Botanist's Journey), 1997–2002

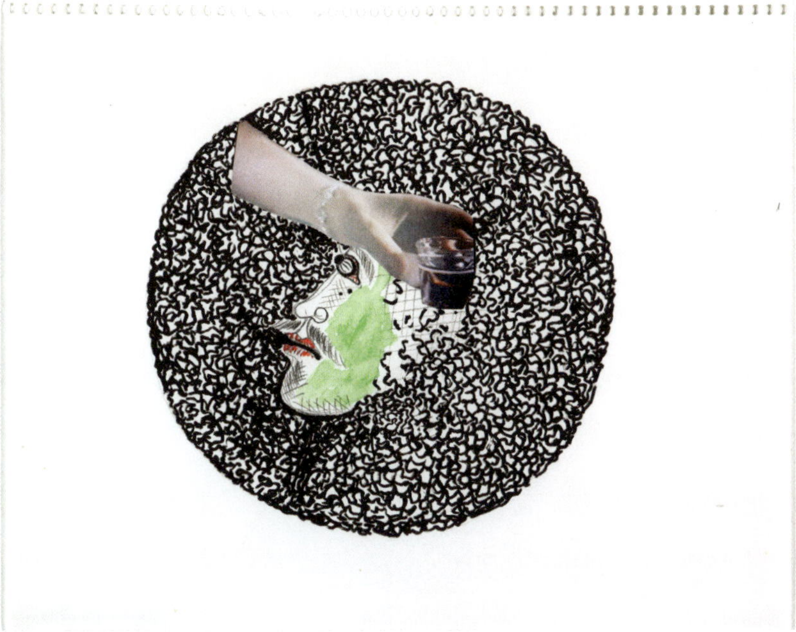

Hallucinogenic Trip from *El viaje del botanista* (The Botanist's Journey), 1997–2002

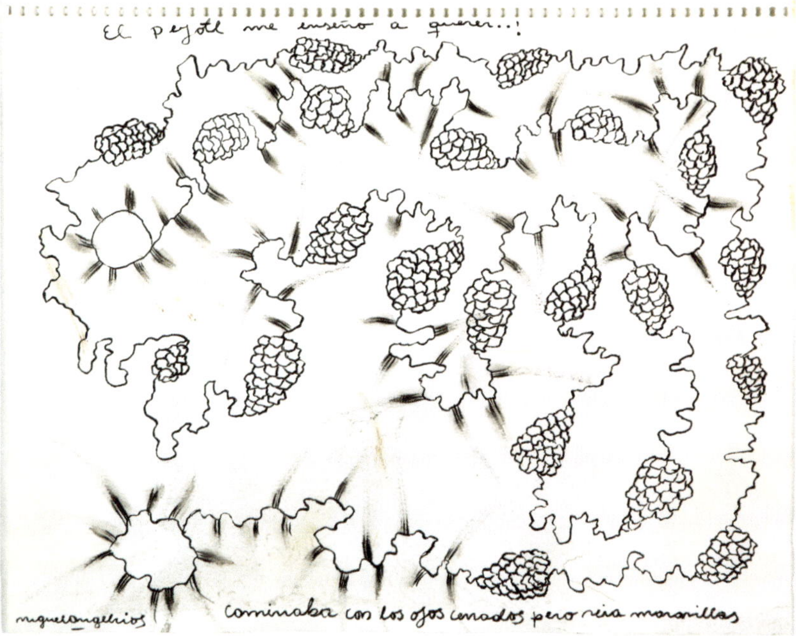

Hallucinogenic Trip #22 from *El viaje del botanista* (The Botanist's Journey), 1997–2002

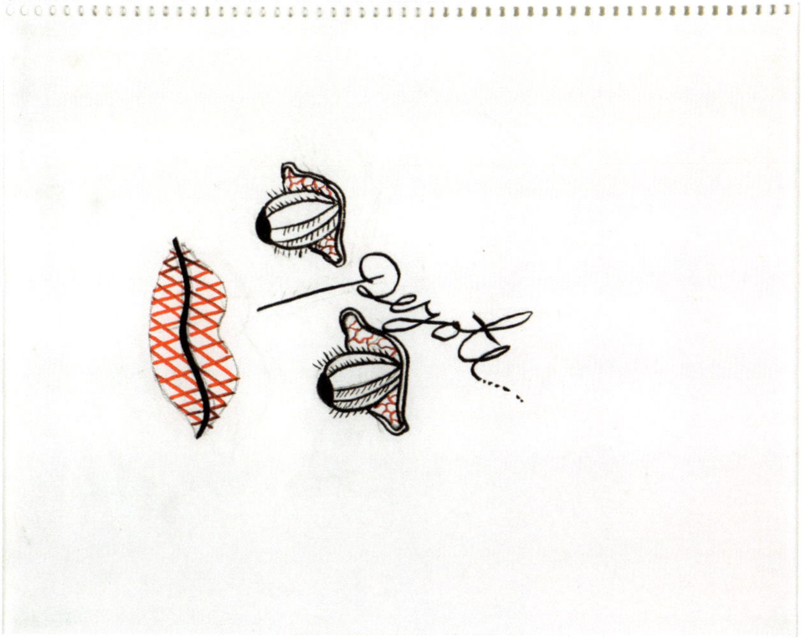

Hallucinogenic Trip #23 from *El viaje del botanista* (The Botanist's Journey), 1997–2002

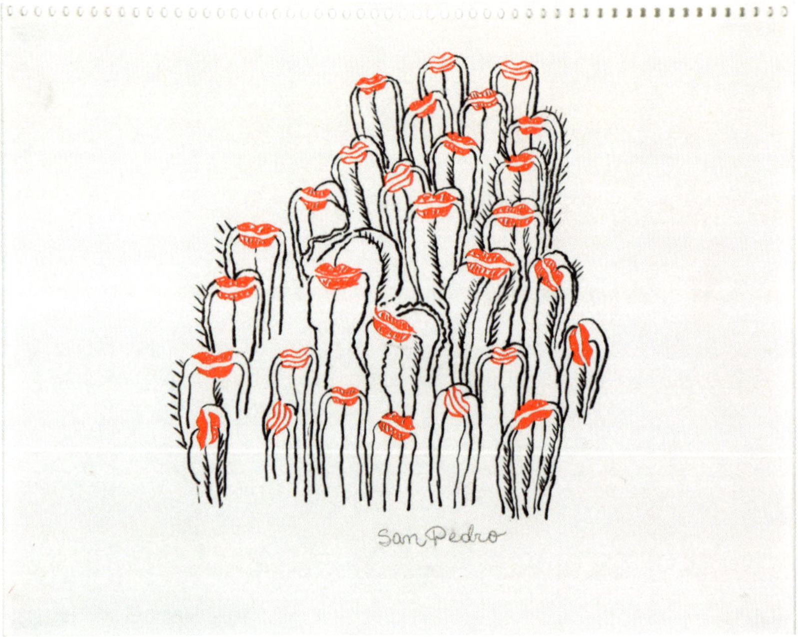

Hallucinogenic Trip #24 from *El viaje del botanista* (The Botanist's Journey), 1997–2002

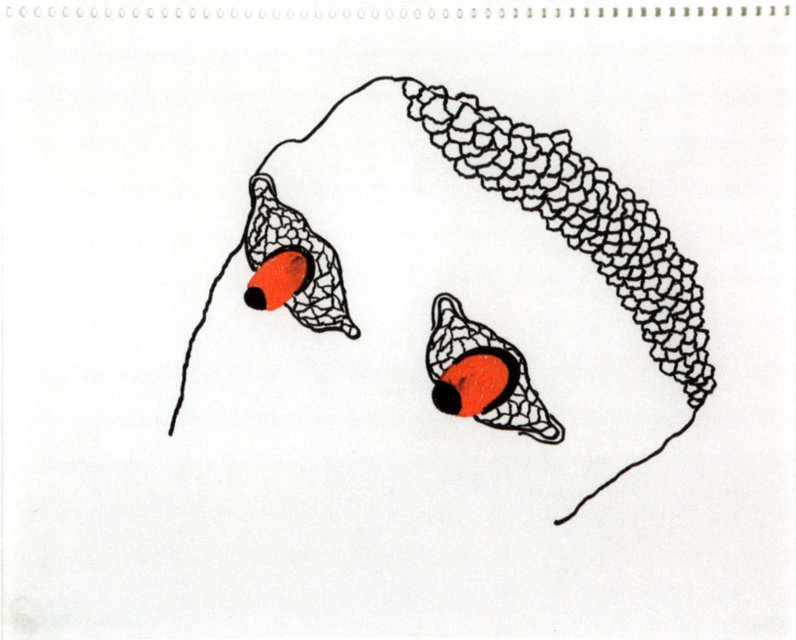

Hallucinogenic Trip #26 from *El viaje del botanista* (The Botanist's Journey), 1997–2002

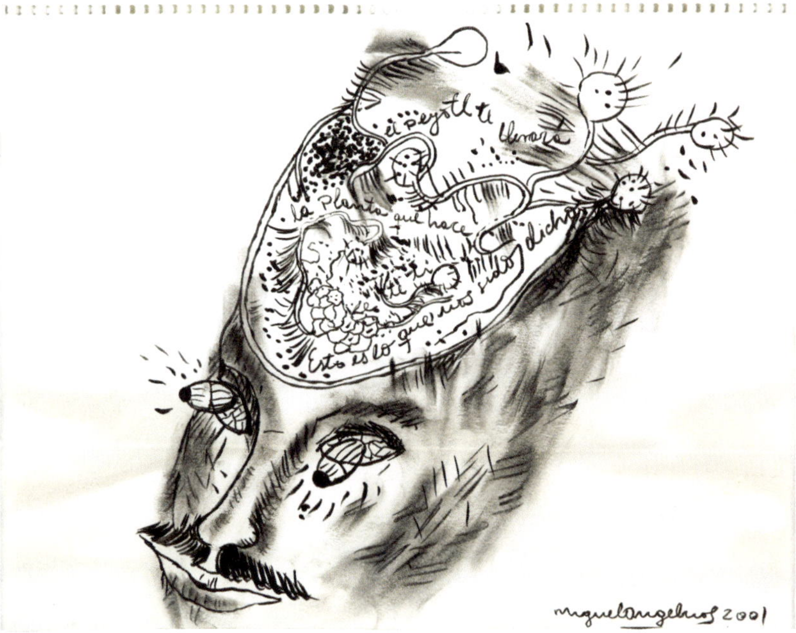

Hallucinogenic Trip #28 from *El viaje del botanista* (The Botanist's Journey), 1997–2002

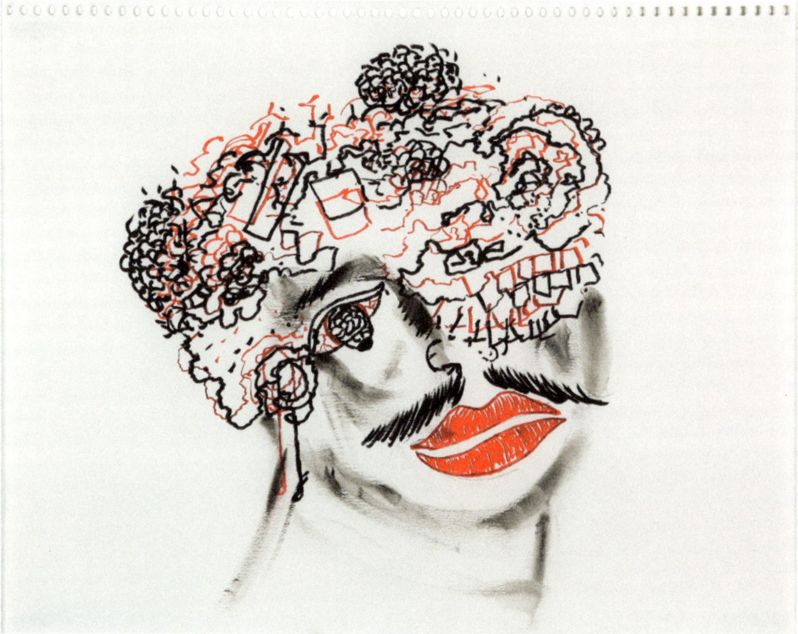

Hallucinogenic Trip #32 from *El viaje del botanista* (The Botanist's Journey), 1997–2002

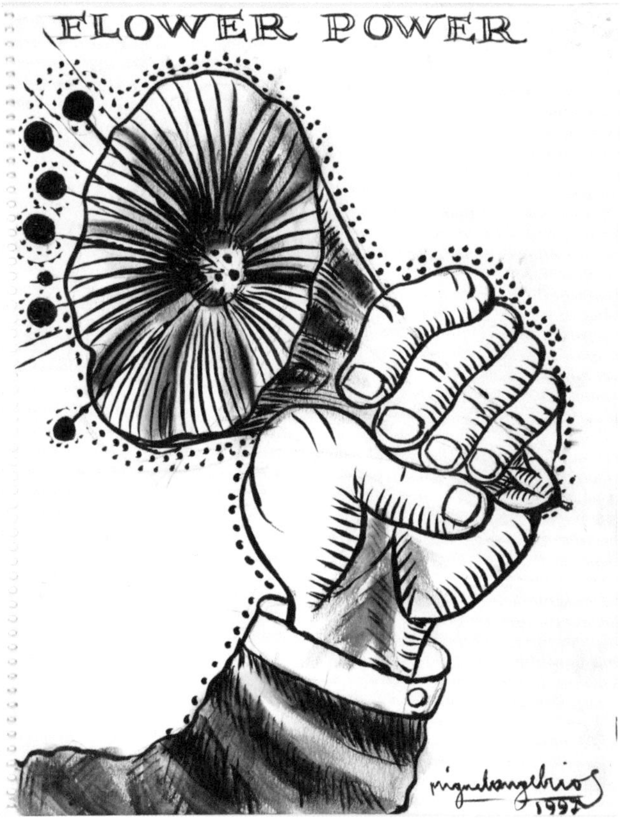

Hallucinogenic Trip #34 from *El viaje del botanista* (The Botanist's Journey), 1997–2002

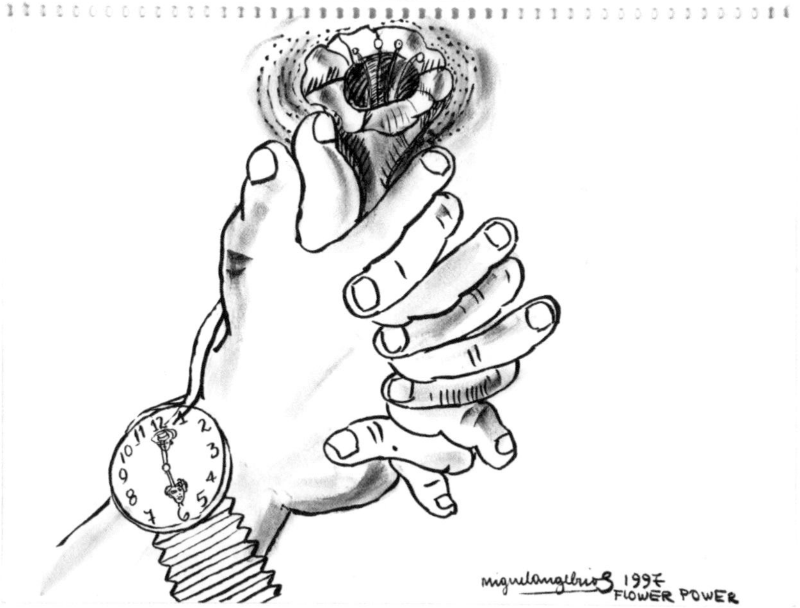

Hallucinogenic Trip #37 from *El viaje del botanista* (The Botanist's Journey), 1997–2002

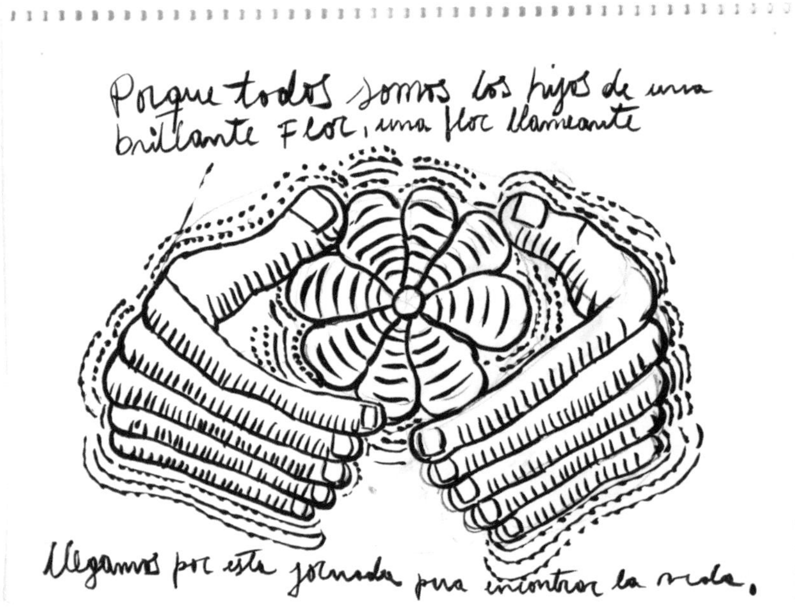

Hallucinogenic Trip from *El viaje del botanista* (The Botanist's Journey), 1997–2002

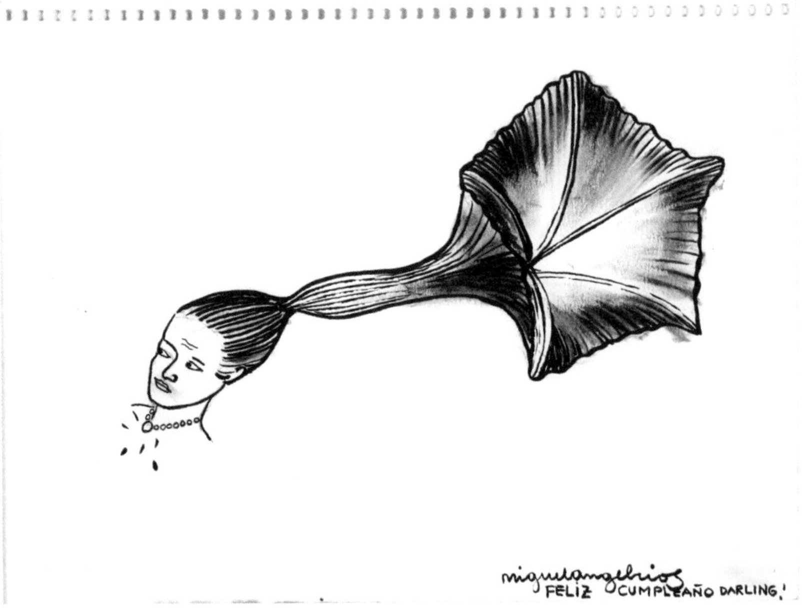

Hallucinogenic Trip #38 from *El viaje del botanista* (The Botanist's Journey), 1997–2002

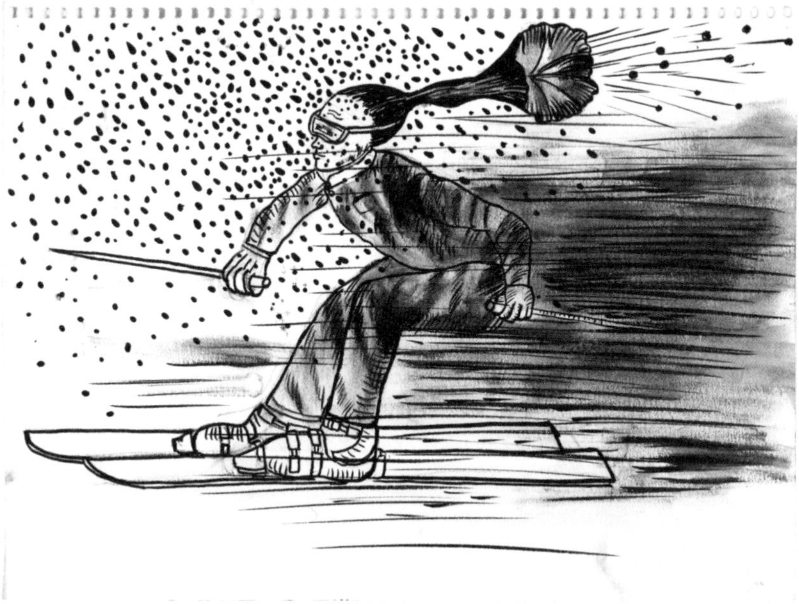

Hallucinogenic Trip from *El viaje del botanista* (The Botanist's Journey), 1997–2002

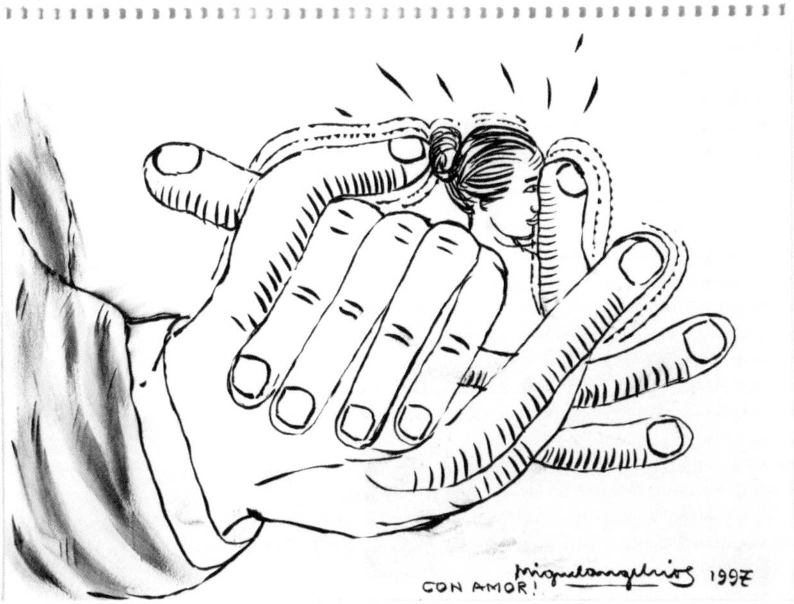

Hallucinogenic Trip #40 from *El viaje del botanista* (The Botanist's Journey), 1997–2002

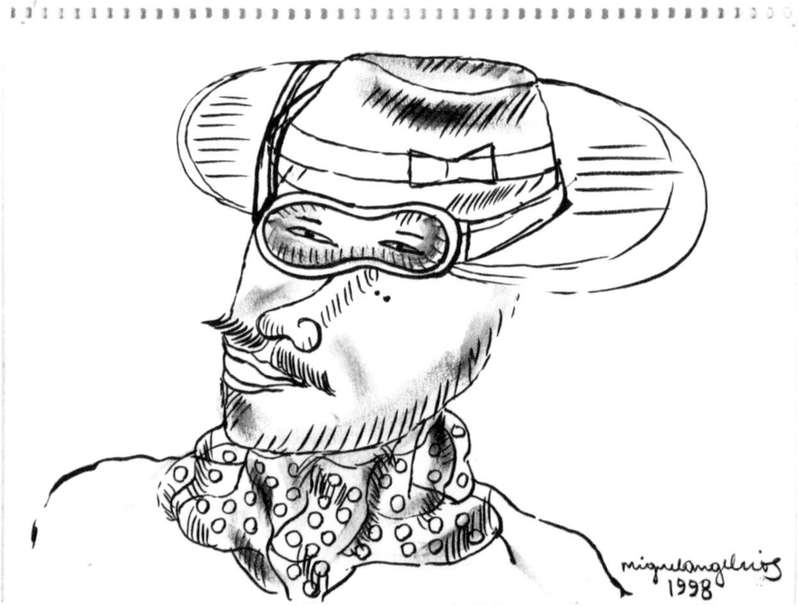

Hallucinogenic Trip from *El viaje del botanista* (The Botanist's Journey), 1997–2002

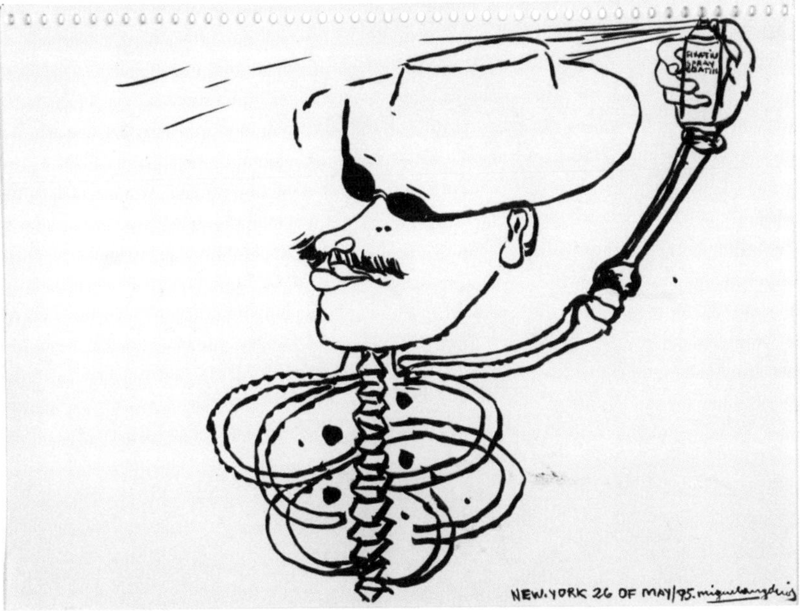

Hallucinogenic Trip from *El viaje del botanista* (The Botanist's Journey), 1997–2002

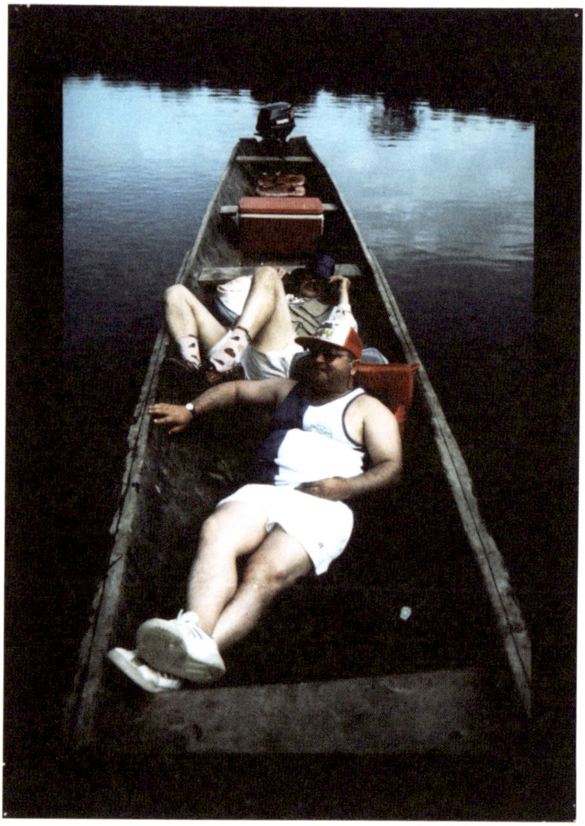

Hallucinogenic Trip from *El viaje del botanista* (The Botanist's Journey), 1997–2002

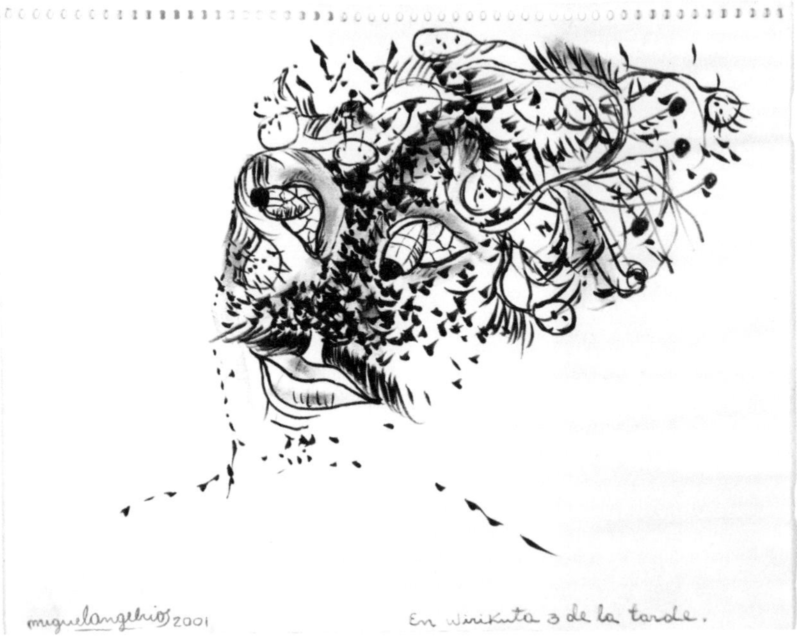

Hallucinogenic Trip #46 from *El viaje del botanista* (The Botanist's Journey), 1997–2002

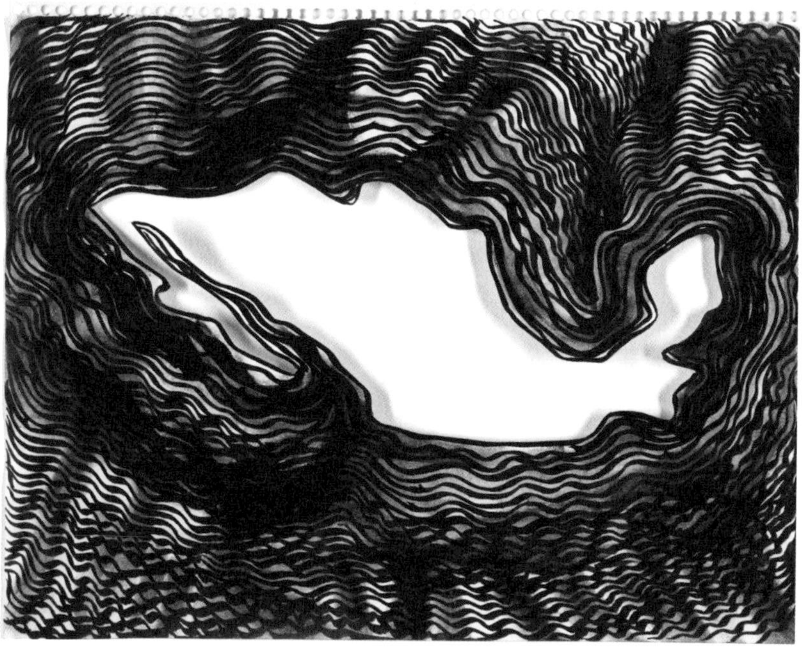

Hallucinogenic Trip #48 from *El viaje del botanista* (The Botanist's Journey), 1997–2002

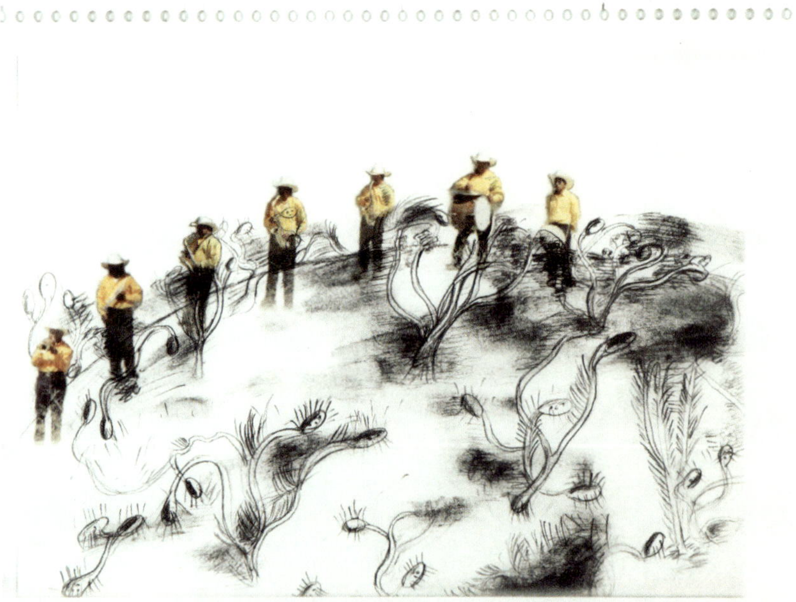

Ni me busques ... No me encuentras (Don't Look For Me ... You Won't Find Me), 2001

hallucinations or fata morganas

by Ruth Estévez

"It was only an illusion! Nothing more.
There is no point in my spirit tormenting me.
There is nothing I can do! ... Nothing I can do at all!"

He sits down and crosses his arms.

The Temptation of Saint Anthony[1]

Someone walks at a quick pace through the Potosí desert. It is a dry steppe that, if we didn't know its precise geographical location, could be any lost place. The camera moves vertiginously and places the viewer in the first person, as if she or he were walking in this random manner. There's panting and a fata morgana vision created by the desert. The screen splits into three parts and further complicates the walk. In a fixed shot, the camera follows the artist, sometimes faster and sometimes slower. The montage of one picture plane after the other follows a single logic that is suggested by the description: pure space (*espacio puro*). Graphically, they weave together in such a way that it becomes difficult to distinguish whether one scene has been shown previously or not.

Ni me busques ... No me encuentras (Don't look for me ... You won't find me), 2002, is Miguel Angel Ríos' first video in which the emptiness and solitude of the desert become the most important scenery. The choice of this landscape is not random. In fact, the dry plateau reappears in several later videos. The space is, undoubtedly, a metaphor for a personal mental state.

The straying protagonist suffers from hallucinations, like a Saint

Anthony in full-fledged ecstasy and under the influence of hallucinogenic herbs. Here, stories from the past and present cultures come together and surface in an indistinct way. When Gustave Flaubert wrote *The Temptation of Saint Anthony*, the hero's canonized self-control and incorruptibility recede into the background. Instead, Flaubert focuses on the cast of characters that attack the defenseless ascetic man, as a way to address the injustices and idiosyncrasies provoked by a violently cultural hybridity. There are sinners—old gods who have been worn out by the triumph of a younger religion, Christianity—as well as strange monsters that symbolize the origin of myth and religion. In *Ni me busques*, the ascetic hero is initiated into a psychedelic trip caused by mushrooms, which morph the temptations into comic though insidious hallucinations. In his altered mental state, Ríos becomes an "other," following the pre-Hispanic tradition of ingesting hallucinogenic plants. This state of otherness that the artist freely enters is a parallel to the notion of the "other," which stems from a colonial, Eurocentric paradigm that determined the understanding of the traditions, behaviors, and overall character of indigenous populations. Ríos uses the narrative of video to avoid such domestication, assimilation, or reduction of these "others," which would allow for their insertion into a nationalist project. His visions, which also appear in a series of travelogue sketches and drawings, interrogate the authoritarian power that uses the disciplining of any kind of otherness as a prime vehicle to organize and control.

Close to the end of the recording, Ríos interrupts the monotony of the walk to enter a stone hut that unfolds into several little rooms. Were it not for the tragic hope that runs through the entire piece, this interlude would have seemed comical. This walk doesn't really have a goal; the only thing to do is to carry on under the influence of the ingested peyote.

Similarly, in *Waiting for Godot*[2], Samuel Beckett uses a desertlike no-man's-land to locate the history of two individuals waiting for a person who never arrives. Here, the absurd also comes to the surface. Yet it is the loneliness of the individuals mixed with the endless waiting, instead of an absurd hidden in surreal visions, that becomes the main character on stage. It is as if the desert were a sort of tabula rasa, a mythical space where everything is possible because the rules of reality and saneness have been suspended. Other rules, those of the artistic framework, are in place. It is the place where the artist (author and/or character in the work) escapes from the world to meditate and reflect about worldly suffering, even if these come back to haunt him.

Nevertheless, there is a fine line between reality and its reflections in Ríos' videos. The imagined may then be reality, and that which we can touch may actually vanish. Whether hallucinogenic visions, extreme changes in the landscape, or the acoustic conditions of those vast empty spaces, they all allow us to perceive things between hallucination and phantasm. The effects that are produced in front of the camera are made in situ (and not in postproduction) and seem like hazy visions. They are an intangible image, either real or imaginary, or simply the rests of a mutilated history. When Werner Herzog filmed *Fata Morgana*[3] in the middle of the Sahara Desert, he showed a quasi-apocalyptic landscape, mirror of a past or future war, whose only prospect was a ruin. The film weaves in passages of the *Popol Vuh*, a sacred text explaining the creation of the universe as well as prophecy of the destiny of the Maya people. Image and text correspond in an abstract way and let the viewers come to their own conclusions. Maybe it is this same uncertainty and confusion that Ríos seeks when he contrasts his psychedelic trip with the desert, letting himself be contaminated by his visions without aiming for redemption or to come unharmed out of the experiment.

II.

Years after *Ni me busques* ... No me encuentras, Miguel Angel Ríos made a series of videos in which the desert is again the prime background. Here, instead of planning a hallucinogenic experiment, the artist used the landscape as the epicenter for a series of visions and auditory experiences that changed the landscape into a full-fledged mirror. In *Rooom, Rooom*, 2010, filmed at the foothills of the Andes, a series of characters carries sticks covered with metallic sheets, which create a strident sound when revolved. Again, the camera dictates the coherence of the video. These sticks, toys of pre-Columbian descent, invade the screen and make the characters disappear. They create a very particular visual effect: Set against the clarity of the recording and the intense blue desert sky, these sticks blind us with a completely unreal optical effect. The sound terrifies the scene, as if it were a soundtrack for a silent movie made afterward.

Here again, total chaos contrasts the peace of the desert landscape. There is no other intention besides finding oneself in the skin of an "other." Actions stay in standby to create confusion and avoid any type of thought that goes beyond sheer unrest. In the sound installation *Meta* (Goal), 2010, a scream of the artist gets lost in the distant mountains that surround the dry Argentine steppe. The scream then returns in the shape of an acoustic dizziness that is contaminated by voices of others. Who shouts? And to whom? The word "*meta*" (goal) is repeated without being able to find a coherent answer. The artist only hears the answer to his own screams through the despair of the echoes—his luck is as ill-fated as the one of the mythical nymph Echo.

In a sense, the desert is a zone of mourning and trial, as if it were a neutral stage on which to reflect about certain present issues. Throughout the filmic discourse and in a very subtle way, the video features a partial view from the side of the subjected, of unattainable proposals, and of minorities with impossible desires, all of which exist as reflections without ever being able to attain a real goal. The contrast between the quiet desert landscape and the artifice purposefully created by the artist is a vehicle to confuse the viewer. The nonlinear narratives also allow one to reflect about other issues, even though they are never clarified. The artist, opposite to Saint Anthony, does not awaken peacefully after having suffered and overcome the temptations. Rather, they stay with him and agonize him in silence while passively waiting for another prodigy to emerge.

1 *The Temptation of Saint Anthony* by Gustave Flaubert, 1874. Flaubert conceived the world as an infernal place in which a series of apparitions occur. Anthony is guided by the devil, who moves around in dreams. Dante's nine circles of hell appear here in the shape of temptations that succeed each other. They are demonic representations of the hermit's own desires that have been created by intellectual curiosity.

2 *Waiting for Godot* (En Attendant Godot), a tragicomedy written in two acts by Samuel Beckett, was first staged in Paris in 1953. In it, two men, who are seemingly homeless, meet at the side of a road in a desolate landscape to endlessly wait for a person called Godot. The disconcerting element in the work is the fact that nothing seems to happen in a constantly repeating cycle in which the meaninglessness of the characters gradually comes to the fore.

3 *Fata Morgana*, released in 1971, was written and directed by Werner Herzog. The work, originally in German, was filmed in the Sahara Desert and accompanied by songs by Leonard Cohen. Fata Morgana stars Lotte Eisner, Eugen Des Montagnes, and James William Gledhill.

Ruth Estévez is Director of LIGA-Space for Architecture-D.F, an interdisciplinary platform for architecture and exhibition practice. She was previously Chief Curator at the Museum of Contemporary Art Carrillo Gil in Mexico City. She has curated exhibitions in Argentina, Brazil, United States, Belgium and Spain and is a regular contributor to Flash Art and Art Nexus.

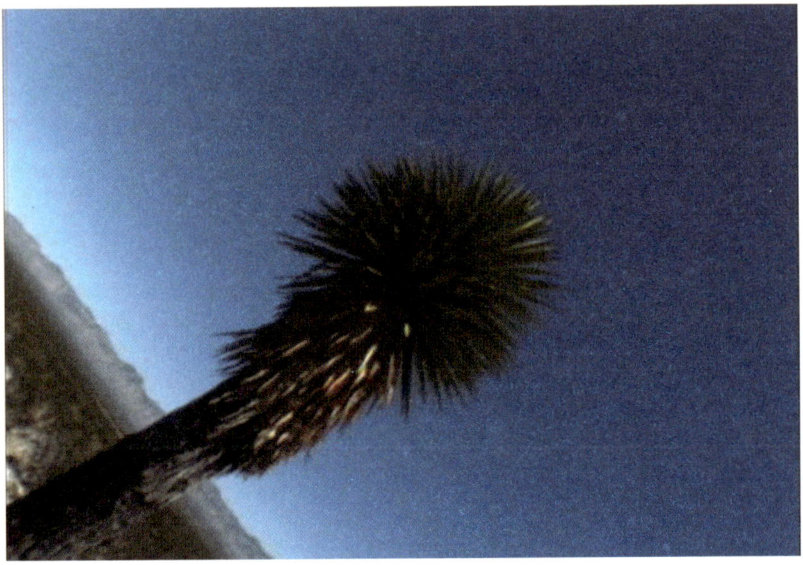

Ni me busques ... No me encuentras (Don't Look For Me ... You Won't Find Me), 2002 (video still)

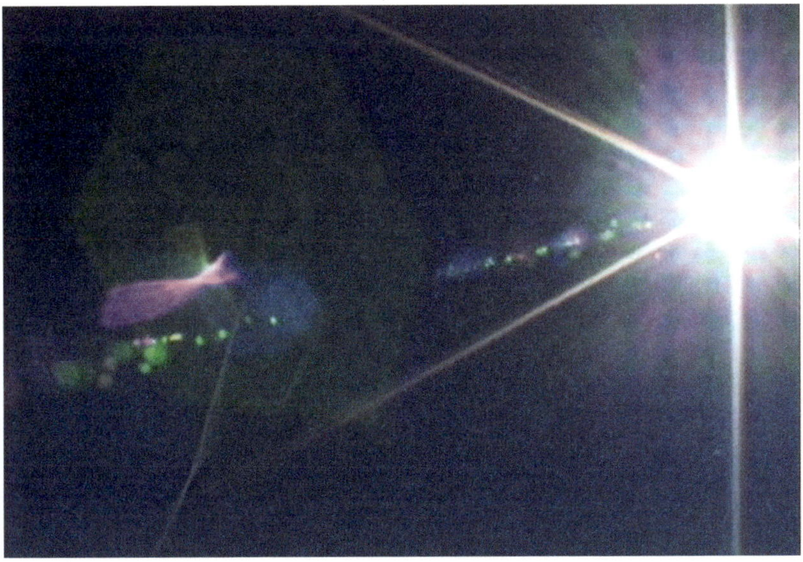

Ni me busques ... No me encuentras (Don't Look For Me ... You Won't Find Me), 2002 (video still)

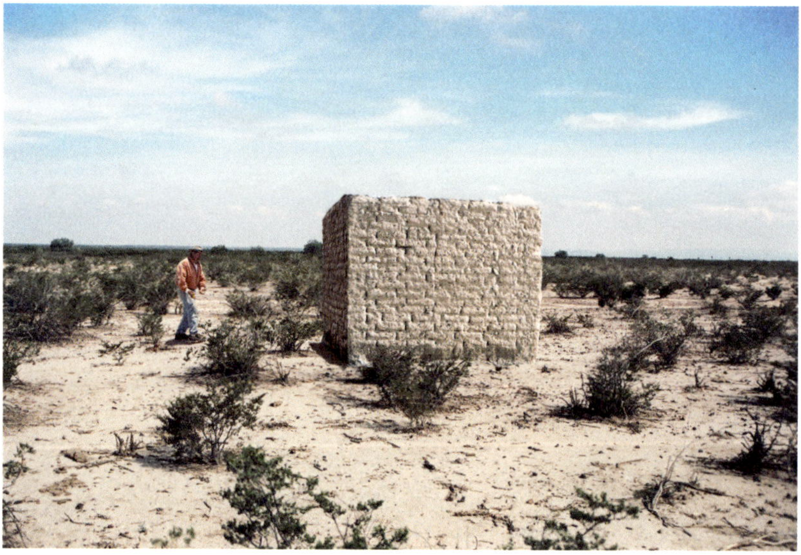

Ni me busques ... No me encuentras (Don't Look For Me ... You Won't Find Me), 2002 (video still)

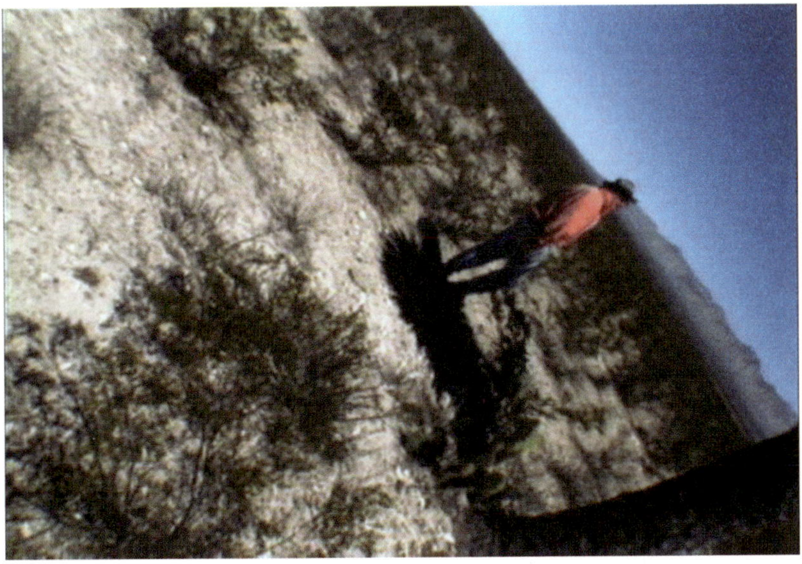

Ni me busques ... No me encuentras (Don't Look For Me ... You Won't Find Me), 2002 (video still)

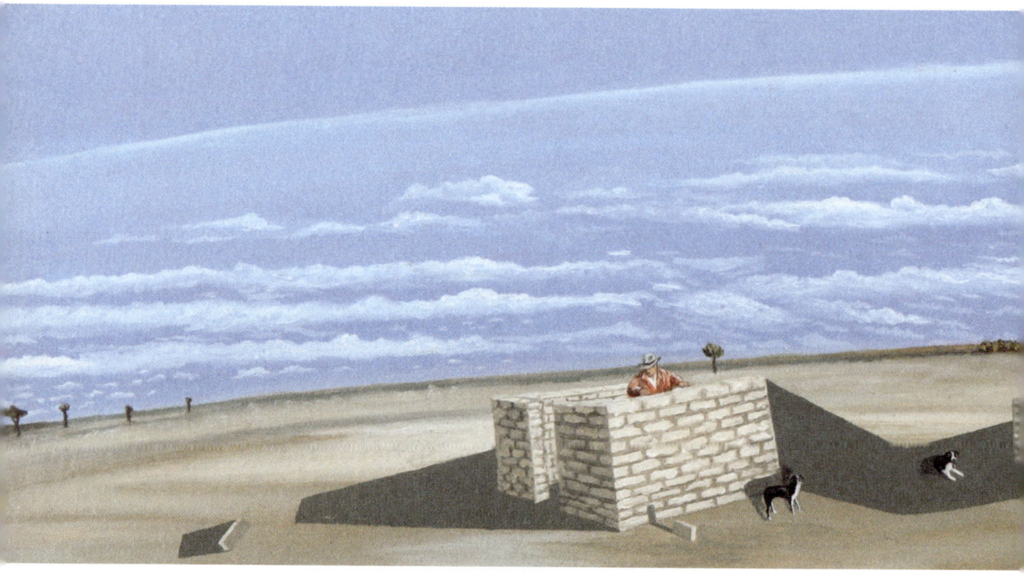

Ni me busques ... No me encuentras (Don't Look For Me ... You Won't Find Me), 2003–2005

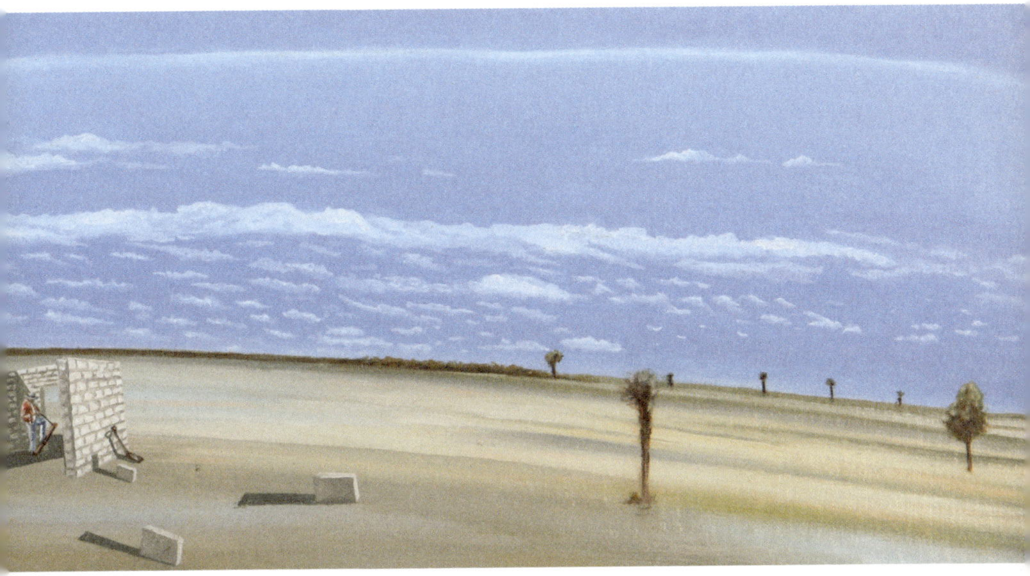

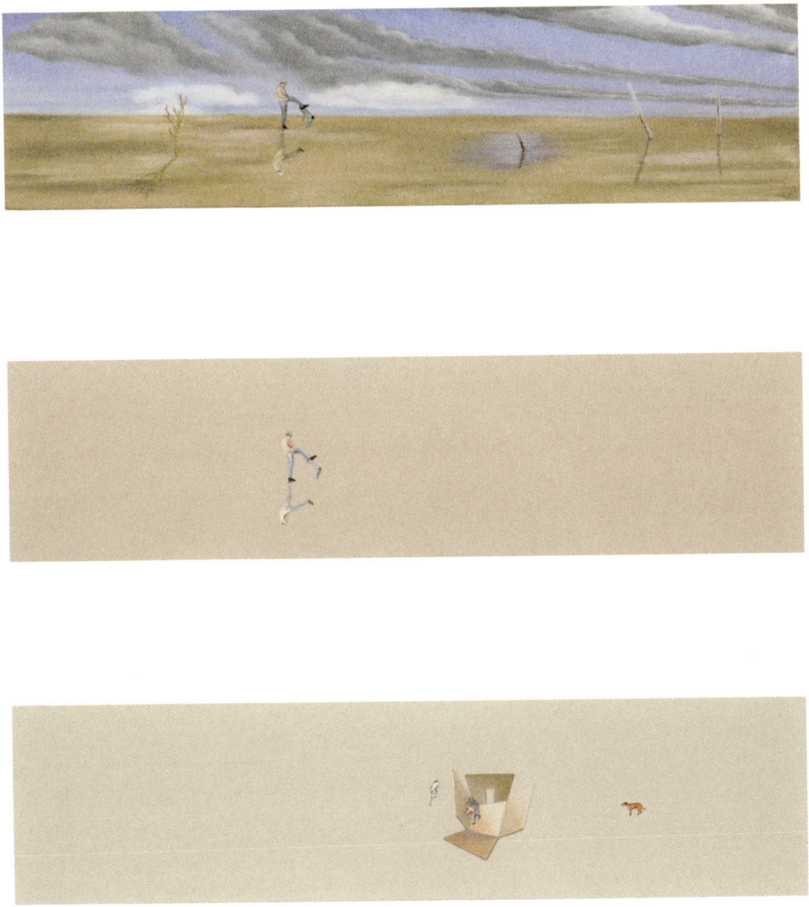

Ni me busques ... No me encuentras (Don't Look For Me ... You Won't Find Me), 2003–2005

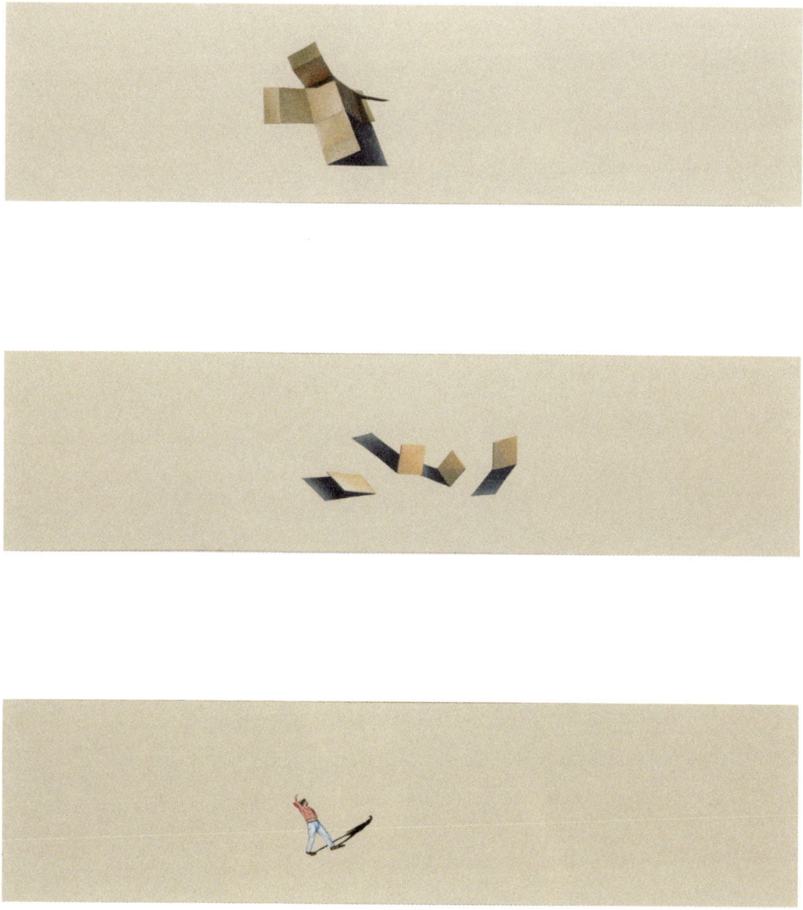

Ni me busques ... No me encuentras (Don't Look For Me ... You Won't Find Me), 2003–2005

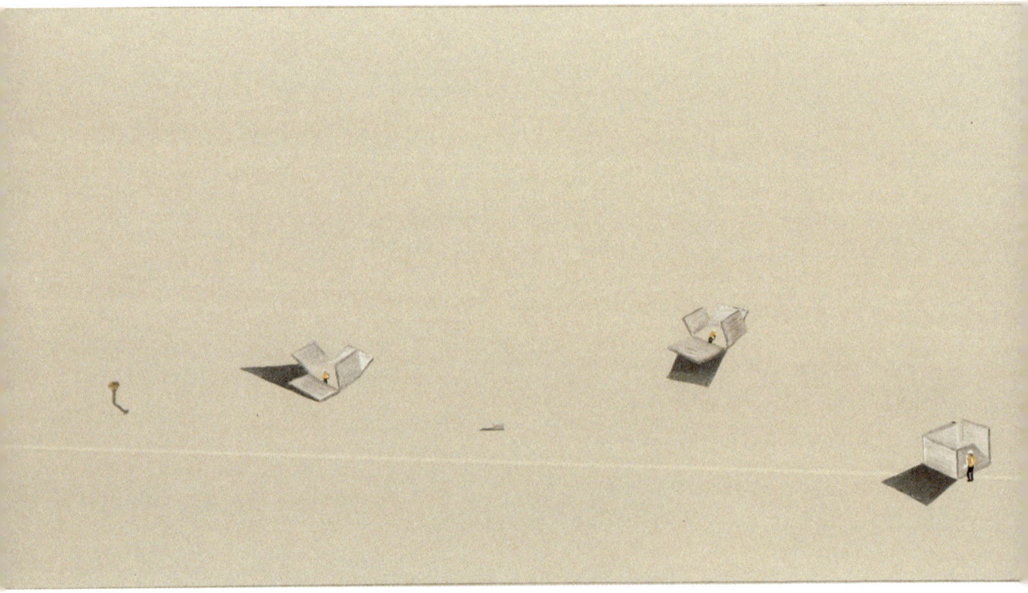

Ni me busques ... No me encuentras (Don't Look For Me ... You Won't Find Me), 2003–2005

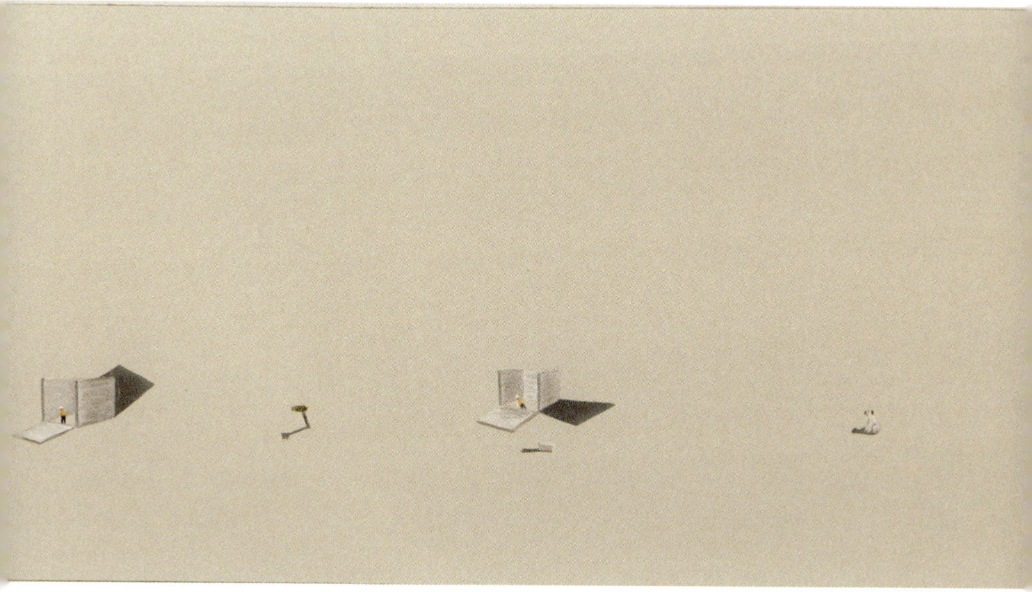

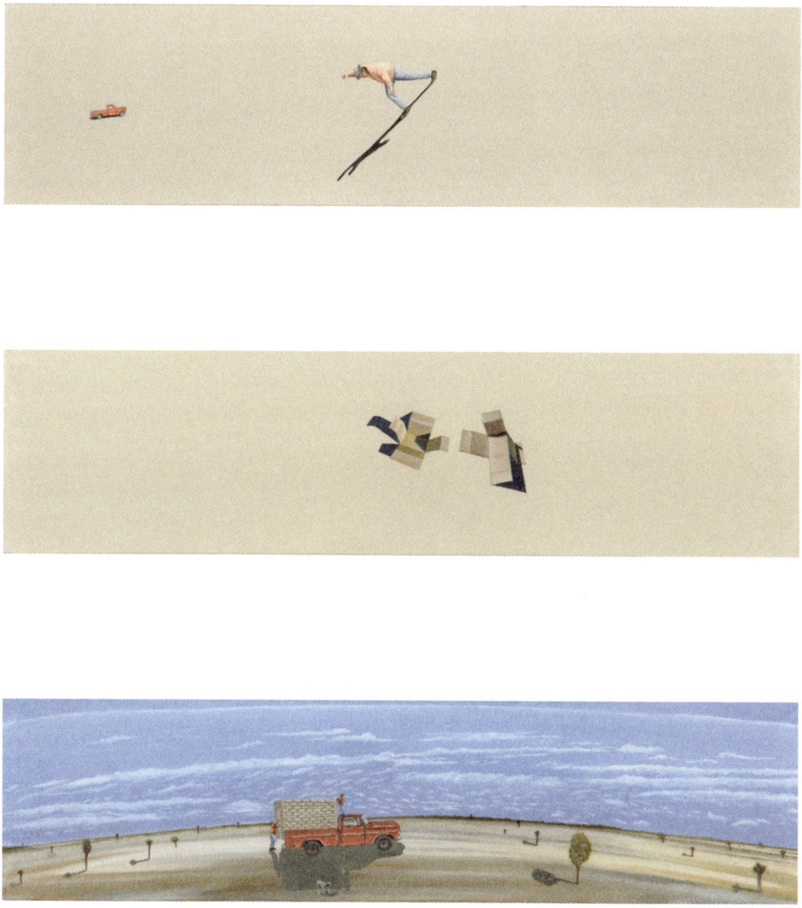

Ni me busques ... No me encuentras (Don't Look For Me ... You Won't Find Me), 2003–2005

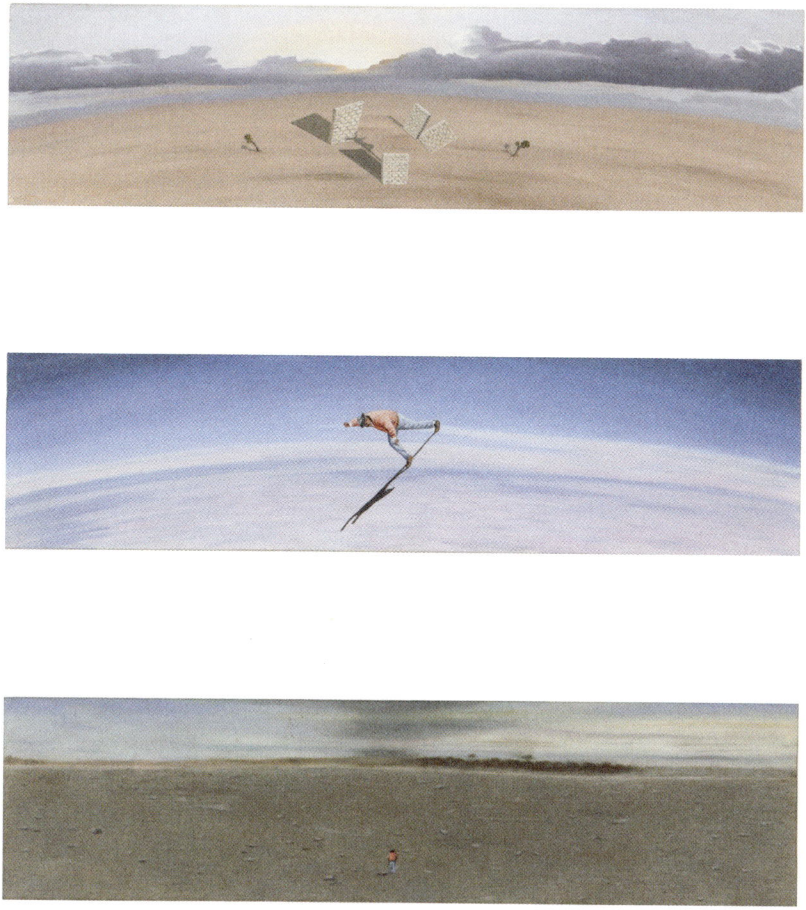

Ni me busques ... No me encuentras (Don't Look For Me ... You Won't Find Me), 2003–2005

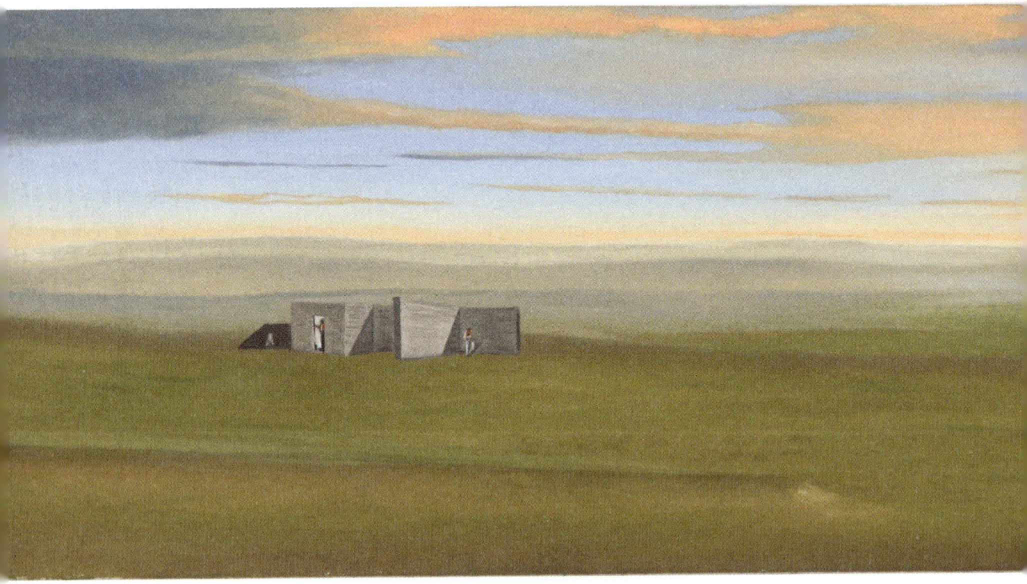

Ni me busques ... No me encuentras (Don't Look For Me ... You Won't Find Me), 2003–2005

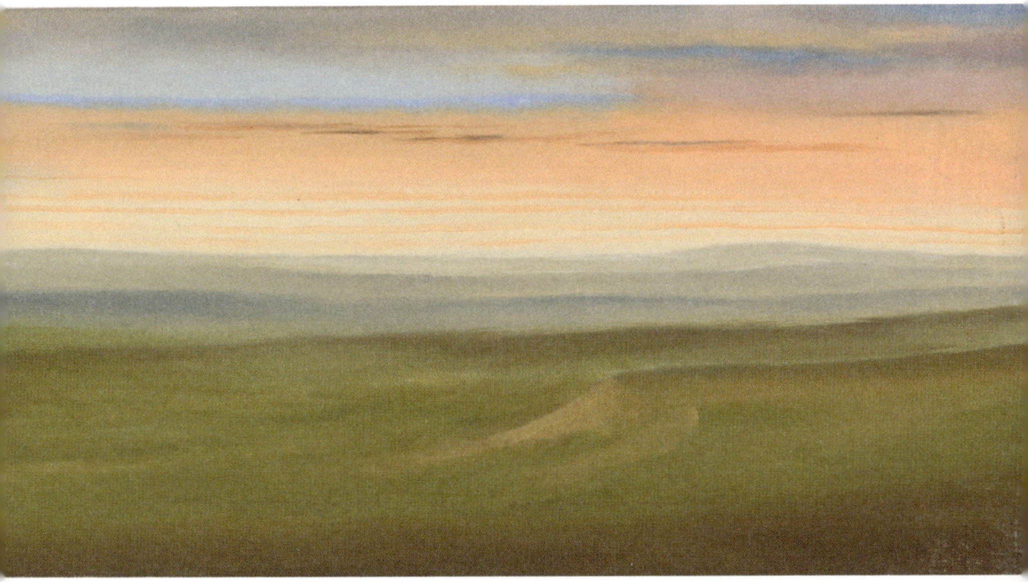

Ni me busques ... No me encuentras (Don't Look For Me ... You Won't Find Me) [detail], 2003–2005

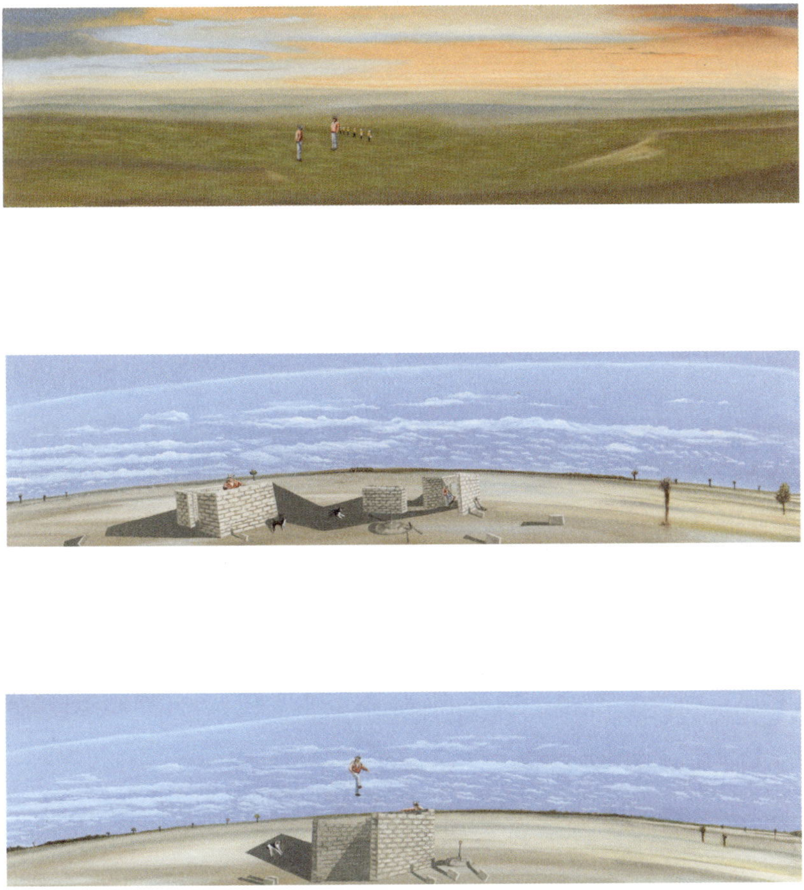

Ni me busques … No me encuentras (Don't Look For Me … You Won't Find Me), 2003–2005

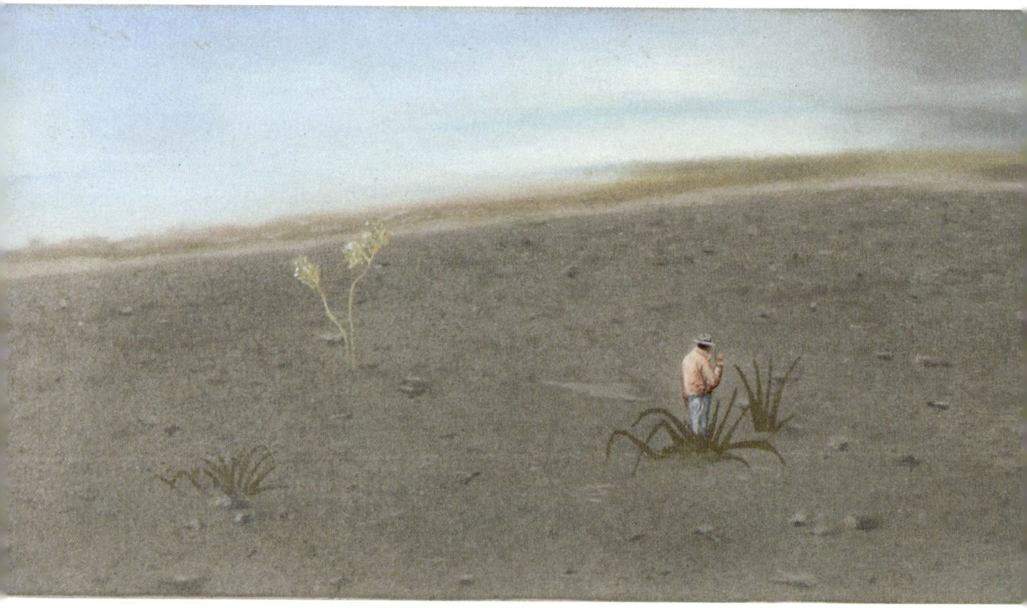

Ni me busques ... No me encuentras (Don't Look For Me ... You Won't Find Me), 2003–2005

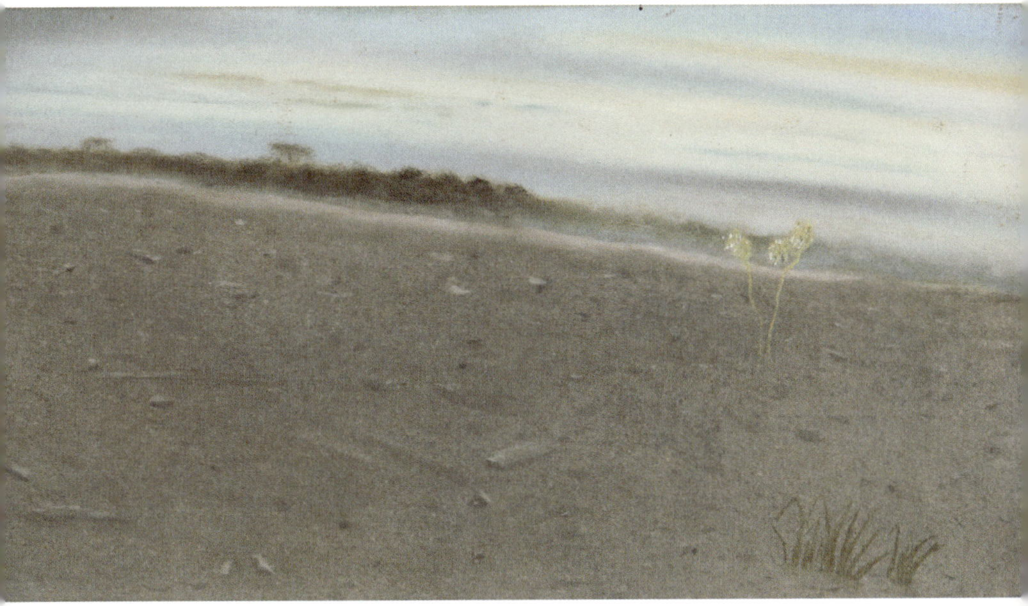

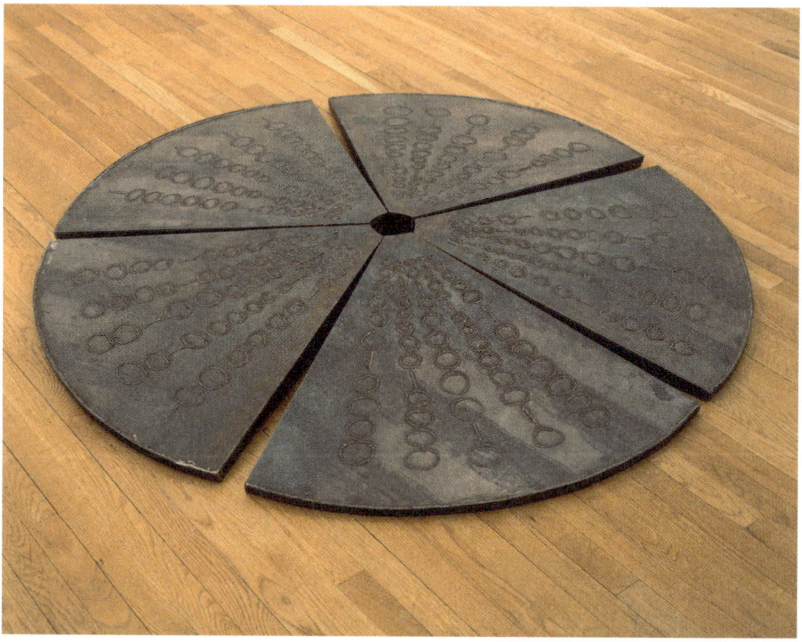

Untitled, 1990. Steel. Collection of Jimmy and Leonora Belilty, Miami, FL

mecha*

by Osvaldo Sánchez

But the regime of the war machine is, above all, that of feelings. [...]
Weapons are feelings, and feelings are weapons.
Deleuze and Guattari.
"Nomadology: The War Machine" in *A Thousand Plateaus.*[1]

KILLING GAMES

Where I come from there wasn't anything, we had to invent games on our own.

Games, whether in the form of their precariously balanced objects or their regulations and organization, have always been latent in Miguel Angel Ríos' work. Recent pieces such as *A Morir* (Till Death), 2003, or *White Suit*, 2008, deal with the transformation of game pieces—or mechanisms—into lethal weapons by way of uncontrolled simulations of the rules of entertainment. These videos can be read as (re)enactments of a mundane ritual of assimilated violence. Their choreography seduces us and we are hooked into a self-sacrificing performance made in reverence to a group that may well be absent. In these pieces, the body itself is diverted, always the toy. The attempt to apply rules to a debt between adults as if it were a game is justified by the difficulty of evoking and enunciating the primordial desire to fully pertain to the group. The artifice of spectacle is conceived of in order to designate its victims, or perhaps to challenge the (im)possibility of their being re-anointed and presented again as an offering.

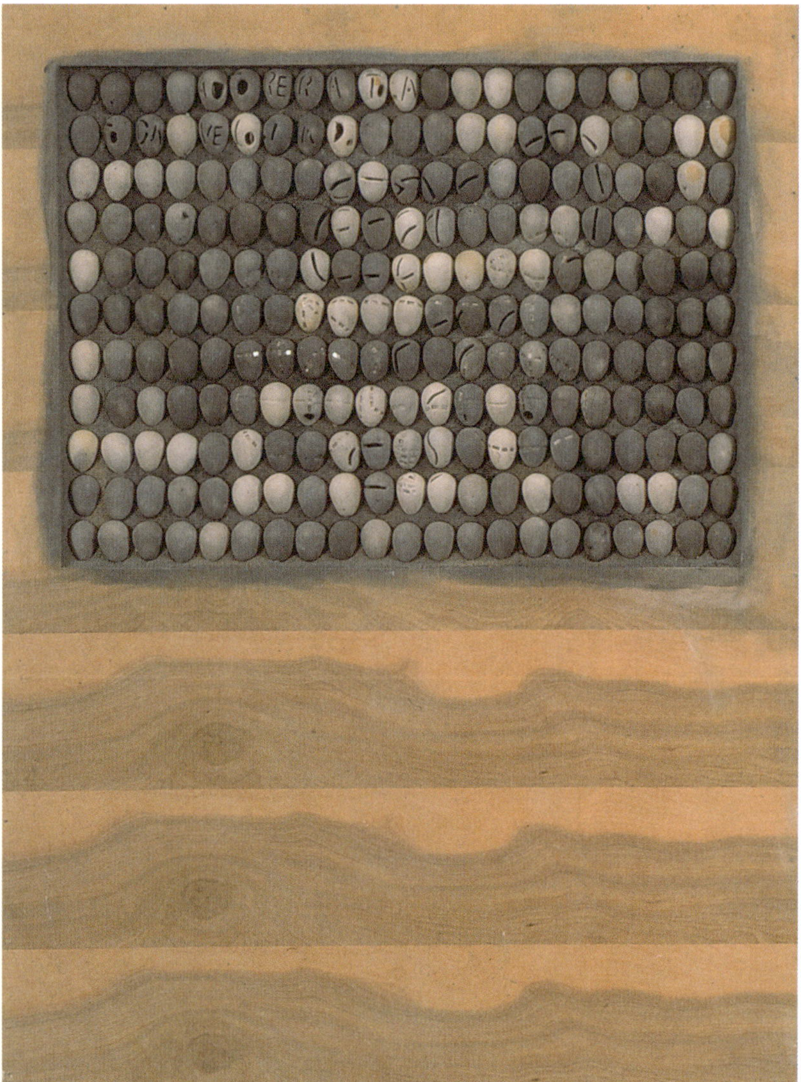

Retablo (Altar), 1988. Clay, mica and wood. Collection of the artist

As a very small child, I became an expert with the boleadoras, *my father taught me. Later, I became invincible with a slingshot. We would go out in groups, from twelve to twenty of us, to the salty bushes to hunt partridge. You had to kill them on their way back, in the air. I never missed. The word got around that little Miguel was an excellent shot. I had competition, the Miravales. And we would make bets, I would go with my group, the Riojas. And even though we would make a stew with the kill, it was all about the sport, it was a killing game.*

As any child knows well, all games, even in their most naïve variations, involve some kind of physical challenge where a niche of the body is exposed as a lesson—or reminder—of the machinery of war. They open up an even expanse where there are no anchors, one wanders nomadically, a preference without a master. The menace of fragility in the face of the elements present in games is an obsession that Ríos has always cultivated in the form of childhood memories.

We also used to shoot these things filled with lead into the air, we would melt it down and we would make boleadoras to hunt the pigeons or parrots that would cross from one ridge to another. It was assassin's play. When you hit them, it transformed you, you would run to catch the animal, before it could hide or before they beat you to it… that's where this pleasure comes from, out of that joy.

It was a trip to Bogotá that facilitated Ríos' contact with the national game called *Tejo*, which, like many popular Latin American games, has its roots in pre-Hispanic traditions[2]. Each individual receives recognition for their skill in throwing a metallic disk that produces an explosion when hitting the target *mecha* from a boisterous, drinking crowd avid for this waste of energy. An ancestral game, its survival may lie in the wisdom of the humorous dynamics of group contact, which maintain a tacit social function today to expel violence.

Tejo *is a dangerous game, played in rough neighborhoods, and it calls for a lot of energy. It always takes place in closed warehouses, in the midst of explosions, the smell of gunpowder and lots of beer. What interested me about the game was the physical energy squandered, the trash, the poverty of the place, the violent atmosphere, mud everywhere, the style of throwing the tejo so that it sticks and the mechas exploding, the fire... it's like war.*

Once again, Ríos worked with the entire arsenal of drama that this game has to offer: its action and codes of conduct, expertise regarding the weapon-artifact, the scene's illusionist potential, the tactile qualities of the materials involved, the acoustic atmosphere of every impact, the secretions at hand... With all this he sets machinery into motion that is increasingly polished in its intentions and engineering, increasingly sadistic in its lethal choreography. The motivational opportunity of pertaining to (or being consecrated within) a group are embodied and put to the test in this game of survival and in the rational or irrational options for interaction. The choreography of animated elements—*tejos*, wheels, shrapnel and spewed mud—constituted as agents or extensions of an invisible command center, deploy an enveloping optical dimension that presents itself to the observing eye as if it were cinemascope. Vision is one of war's coordinates, a digital sight without fixed margins in perpetual movement. The *tejos* fly with the precision of Ninja stars guided by high-fidelity sensors, they cut through the air and stop, with a brief *rallenti* before exploding, suggesting a bullet time dimension. The wooden wheels expand the territory, they charge toward us like robots, like Trojan horses or remote-controlled armored vehicles. The warehouse, a condensed rectangle of smoke, becomes a battlefield without heroes. Any orifice is an eye that sees. The entire *povera* setting takes on a tragic dimension in its high performance "military artifacts", carriers of the drive to (re)inscribe ourselves socially as *spectacle*. The mud is more fluid and it spews and splashes, splattering the lens with the interdiction of the recently secreted. Mud takes on the tragic density of blood itself.

I came from an adobe house.

Those who make the best mechas are considered maestros; their identity is quasi clandestine and we never see their faces. *I said to him: let's see, make an explosion that sends that stone four meters into the air...* The players are faceless and bodiless; their subjective possibilities are made manifest through their prosthetics. They would seem to "act" like computers, making "...all the repetitions function" (Deleuze), imposing a vitality that consists of collisions... or perhaps "a law of electromagnetic proximity"? (Virilio)

There are really hard [playing] fields. Whole blocks of fields. There can be up to 1500 people on the fields... Lots of the people who play are used to hard work, and in the process of taking tejo to the limit, they know how to take risks, to push the line where violence is unleashed. It's a game that sends you home relaxed, as one of the clan.

As in French, in Spanish there is only one word—*juego*—to designate the specificities and differences present in the words game and play in English; the difference between randomness or the existence of rules, between aptitude and the mechanism itself. In Spanish, both Game and Play are always *juego*. This piece by Ríos operates in the interstices between both models of social contact and inscription: on the one hand, it makes up the way in which a game transgresses its own norms; on the other, it turns the visual record and its models of reality into a malleable, corruptible and easily demystified development process. The parodied construction of the 'game' is manipulated as a function of a scenario whose imagery defies 'play'.

ALTARS...

The events in Ríos' videos always underline the negated presence of a fourth theater wall. Vision is cloistered and details controlled as they are in the scene of a ritual. In *Mecha*, the stage-box is more psychedelic and would almost seem to suggest a (mental?) cubicle—container of emotions/container of weapons—delineated by indicators of vectors and energy from the realm of particles and fields.

Certain arithmetic progressions present in Ríos' early works would seem to explain the interest in the mechanized dynamics of

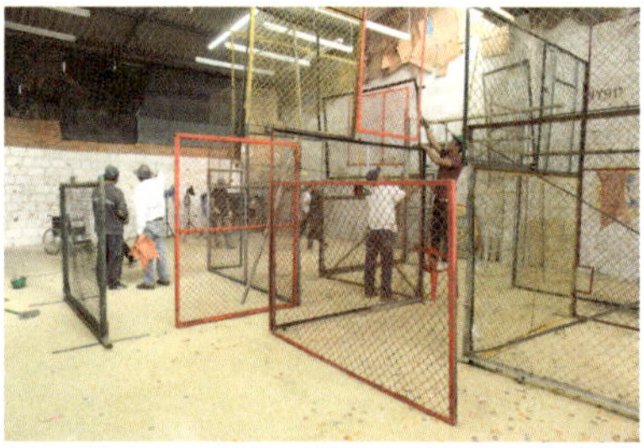
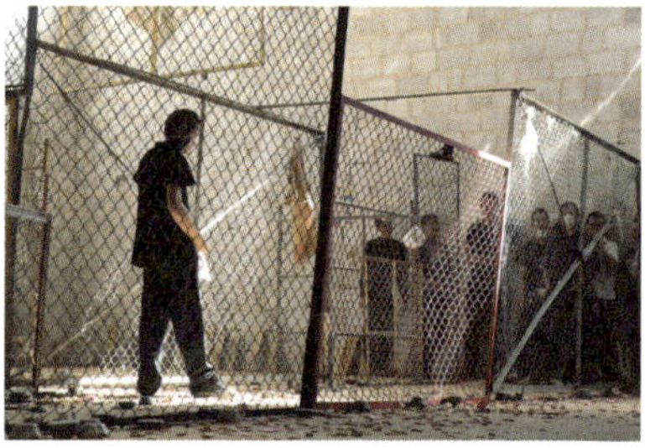
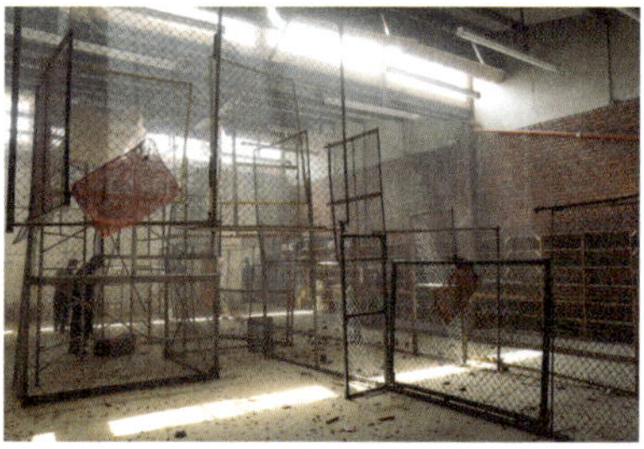
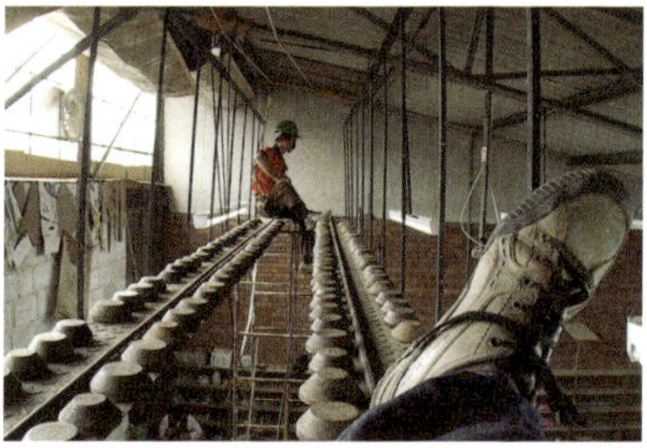

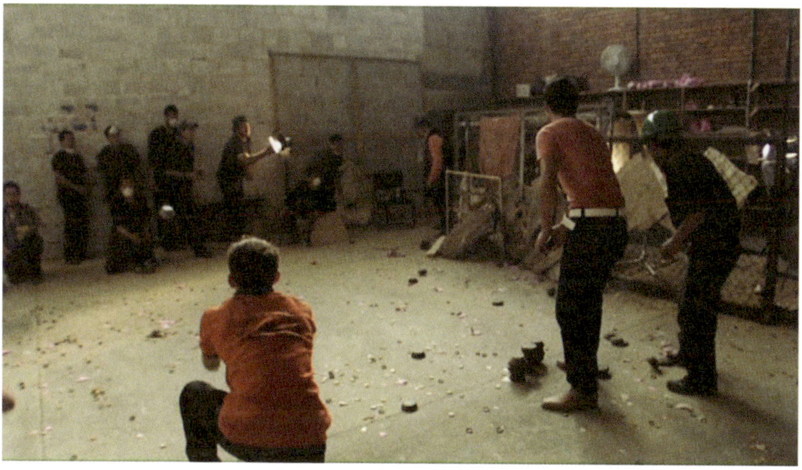

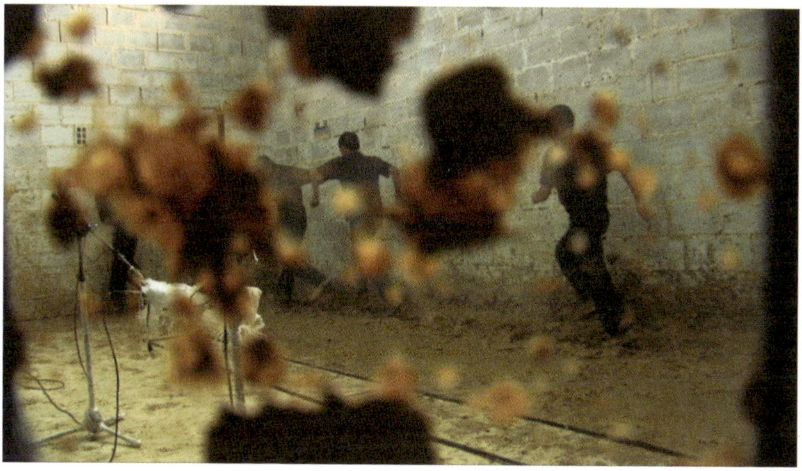

Production stills from *Mecha* (Fuse), 2010

his first videos, his focus on almost robotic choreography and the secret process of development of certain multiplied orders; in *Mecha*, all these things acquire the precise, fictional key of an image simulation laboratory. His handling of mobility at play and his visual organization of space by way of combat accessories-factors design an optical "chip" capable of introducing us to a kind of "telemetric reality". It is a *staging* established within the logic of secrets and vigilance. Traditional parameters of aesthetics can hardly endorse the "live realism" of this new context, machined between human extensions and—possibly—sensors and panels for tracking and control. The devices' sculptural primitiveness contrasts with the cybernetic illusion of the register. (And Ríos builds up this claustrophobic, anxiety-ridden vision through editing and the paranoid binocularity of the double screen.)

Close-ups in the video unfold like a diorama of war. The behind-the-scenes view—from where a spectator (soon omniscient victim) awaits—grants the condition of superimposed screen to that which is observed: a diorama effect, designed to be seen through a lens. At first, such illusionism depends primarily on the handling of light and superimposed shots... but soon everything takes on the continuous, vertiginous circularity of a cinemascope. And it is in this vertigo that the spectator discovers him or herself victim. It is a revelation that recalls Gary Hill's phrase: *Vision is no longer the possibility of seeing, but the impossibility of not seeing*. These progressions of optical systems—ranging from binocular perspective to three-dimensional movements that act as panopticons in check—de-territorialize the scene and situate the spectacle of violence *in crescendo* inside a chronosphere.

A meticulous (de)construction of the images as stills allows us to confirm many surprisingly evident formal analogies between Ríos' earliest works in painting, sculpture and three-dimensional wall object pieces and the formal repertoire of *Mecha*. This is clear in its self-contained box (or Chinese boxes within boxes), in the accumulation of ovoid shapes or disks that can almost be manipulated, the predominance of sepia or a monochromatic range, and an interest in transferring the iconographic impact of the serial to the dimension of time. This already appears in 1992, explained in a text by John Yau for *Der Brücke*, in which he describes Ríos' structural solutions as "a box inside another box..." . He also speaks of his obsession with series and accumulation as devices; in the *kipus* and the multiple planes with abstract symbols derived from code with which "... the artist frames a vision of time".[3]

WE, THE REPLICANTS...

We had fought in wars not yet dreamed of... in vast nightmares still unnamed. We were the new people [...] We were made for this world.
Deckard, *Blade Runner* (Ridley Scott, 1982)

At some moment something explodes, the lens goes blurry and we can sense the reporter's body sink, grope about in the dark, and we hear him die, slowly. There is a blind moment in the register of any war. It is there in *La Batalla por Berlín* (1945), and in Neil Davis' shorts, in *Paralelo 17* by Joris Ivens (1968)... And sometimes, the one recording isn't a hero prepared to die, but a machine with a viewfinder, poised on some distant satellite. Through sudden vibrations of frequency or light, a digital scale model narrates a massacre with no apparent tragedy, without any subjects in view. We've all seen it on TV, the phosphorescent trajectory of drones in the Gulf War. *Tejos* zip across the screen, perforating the slabs, blowing hollows of smoke into the mucky clay. The reticular implosion of detail reinforces the pornographic dimension of this spectacle of violence. The terrain of the game is precisely that no man's land where subjective concerns and life in common intersect; the outside world and the inner realm (Dauvignard). Spatters of mud block the lens. The effect recalls Hans Namuth's film on Pollock. The splash: emotions adrift, unable to find a recipient. As in that transcendental record of Pollock's gestures in the act of dripping, in this case the "pictorial" paste splattered on the crystal screen emphasizes the ritualistic, performative nature of an (abstract) expression of energy.

When I was young I used to dance malambo a lot, and later contrapunto... You had to improvise without missing a beat.

The double image/screen is one of the devices that allow us to answer back in the face of occasionally contradictory narrative models of register. At certain moments, these choreographies take on the quality of a scene put on pause. At others, they might be the replay of a backup version of events, or a synchronized record, coverage of zapping. All the visions allude to different models of tracking and (re) presentation generated by technological implants. They suspend time, they are capable of leaving us disoriented in our usual estimates of time's duration (Virilio), with a temporality made up of simulated *ritornellos* and geophysical indications. This spatial-temporal drain in his video pieces—most emphatically in *Mecha* and *Rooom Rooom*—refers back to two key sources in Ríos' lived experience: his artistic itinerary through abstraction with spiritual references and his experimentation with natural psychotropic substances to incite para-real visions/revelations.[4]

FRAGILE SUBJECTS. DEMAND.

I was a kid from the provinces, timid, but very street-smart... Later I worked in the Post Office, designing stamps. They fired me because I drew a San Martín with really big ears.

He who fears is all eyes. His vision is reinforced by the fatigue of a body-organ that breathes, heaving, dragging itself into the background in stealthy retreat. An animal sensed in the dark, it only looks for the chance to survive.

We would situate ourselves in the middle of that enormous, square mountain. The rest would throw big, white stones trying to hit us, and we would have to run.

This is contempt for the failed hero on the part of the other witnesses. However, behind the fourth wall there is no one to accompany you, there doesn't seem to be any public; circuits, perhaps, the rest of the machine of which we form a part. And on this stage—where you might at times sense the fleeting gesticulation of a cyborg—the eye of a phantom body-organ, vigilantly panting in the dark, is focused on comprehending its own imminent defeat. It is the centrifugal domain of desire—with seduction as a *production of distance* (Virilio)—over fear's centripetal vertigo. It is an ancestral violence whose argument is the sacrifice of he who is observed observing, chosen for an unfamiliar ritual. This isolation of the subject on the battlefield of war may well be an accusation of the current cannibalization of what we used to call a *collective past*. Today, it is something only spectacle can convoke.

The victim, whose identity as a target is omniscient, is exposed to a devouring, centripetal scenario. Alone. And this is because the landscape is all machinery. Landscape is the measure of he who exposes himself to the shot. In these halls of vision, the hero's possibility of gaining access to his own heroicness, his offering to the public, slips away (*The Matrix*, Wachowski Bros., 1989). The mechanism of the game and its game piece-toys are *transitional fetishes* that oblige participation in fictions, in shady cognitive experiences that take us into another time of the self. Recognition of the toy in "its disguised intention of being accepted as a gift, [...] implies submission: the child dominated by the adult".[5]

We went to the jungle. And in the distance, with binoculars, we could see the prisoner's feet.

The presence of those feet, whether bussed in or convinced, turns the game—or the image simulator—into a public act. There is a nod to corporate authority's robotic structure of mediation. The rushed steps of agents—Smith, Brown or Jones, from *The Matrix*—function as the coryphaeus' text, who, marching toward the inevitable, amputates the hero's emotional opportunities as he pushes forward.

The angst here also comes from not being able to recognize any centralized model of authority in the occurrences. That would require some chink of subjectivity in the machine, some fissure of desire amidst the gears. *Do you love me? Do you trust me?* Always, the same desire to offer one's self up...

And losing, at times, is a demand.

"– Smell that? You smell that?
– What?
– Napalm, son. Nothing else in the world smells like that."
Kilgore/Lance, *Apocalypse Now* (Francis Ford Coppola, 1979).

* Translator's note: *Mecha* (literally "fuse") in the context of the sport of *Tejo* refers to a folded paper triangle filled with gunpowder.

1 Deleuze and Guattari. "Nomadology: The War Machine" in *A Thousand Plateaus*. Ed. De Minuit. Paris, 1980. p. 498....

2 *Tejo* is Colombia's national sport and it is played by throwing a metal plate or disc, called a *tejo*, at a target consisting of an inclined bed of clay at the far end of an 18-meter long field in order to strike the "mechas" and make them explode. The game was originally practiced by the Chibcha people from pre-Hispanic central-Western Colombia over 500 years ago, who used a disc of gold called a "zepguagoscua" weighing approximately 680 grams. As the game became more popular, the "zepguagoscua" was replaced with a stone disc and today, a metal disc (*tejo*) of the same weight is used. The idea of the game is to toss the *tejo* so it lands within the "*bocin*", a steel cylinder embedded in the clay on the borders of which the "*mechas*" are placed. Whoever explodes the greatest number of *mechas* or manages to land the *tejo* in the *bocin*. Either individuals or teams compete. Scoring is are agreed upon between rivals, although in the majority of cases is as follows: All players make their throws and the *tejo* closest to the *bocin* gains a point (*mano* or hand), and is the one to begin throwing in the next round. Three points or *manos* equal a *balazo*, the name for burning a *mecha*. Games tend to be arranged mainly on the basis of *balazos*. Landing the *tejo* in the *bocin* is called *embocinar* and is equivalent to two *balazos*. The highest scoring toss is when the *tejo* explodes a *mecha* and also lands inside the *bocin* in one throw, and this is called a "*moñona*", equal to three *balazos*. Another variation is known as mini-*tejo*, which is the same as the larger version but in smaller proportions. Only one *mecha* is put in place and whoever makes it explode wins the most points. In both cases, the game is played in fields that face one another. Whoever winds up closest to the *bocin* throws first, and so on. (Wikipedia)...

3 John Yau. *Miguel Angel Ríos*. Ed. Die Brücke ediciones. Colección Cuadernos de Arte. Buenos Aires, 1992...

4 There is another, similar contrast between the type of technologized vision/knowledge that is parodied and the poor infrastructure of the pieces' production process. It is not only in the intimate format of the staff, or in the active inclusion of the player-actors in the technical solutions and improvisation of the rudimentary apparatus; but also in the precarious budget sustaining the entire production. Dollies and traveling shots were resolved by way of assembling pulleys and twine, and filming relied on risky acrobatics on the part of the assistants. A meticulous storyboard was continually taken over by happy accidents. Players' collaboration was undoubtedly with an understanding of how violence derives, based on the credibility of the marks it leaves behind. These players have a tough training as witnesses, victims and victimizers that is very present in the filming's rarified fidelity...

5 Jean Duvignaud, *El juego del juego*. Ed. FCE. Mexico, 1982. p. 46]... [Paul Virilio. *The Aesthetics of Disappearance*. Ed. Anagrama, Barcelona, 1988. / *La vitesse de libération*. Ed. Galilée. 95, Paris. / *Un paysage d'évenements*. Ed Galilée. 96.]

Osvaldo Sánchez is an art critic and curator. He is currently Director of the Museum of Modern Art in Mexico City. Previously he was Artistic Director for the 2005 edition of InSite/Artistic Practice in the Public Sphere in Tijuana – San Diego. He has also held directorial positions at the Museum of Contemporary Art Carrillo Gil and Museum of Contemporary Art Rufino Tamayo, both in Mexico City.

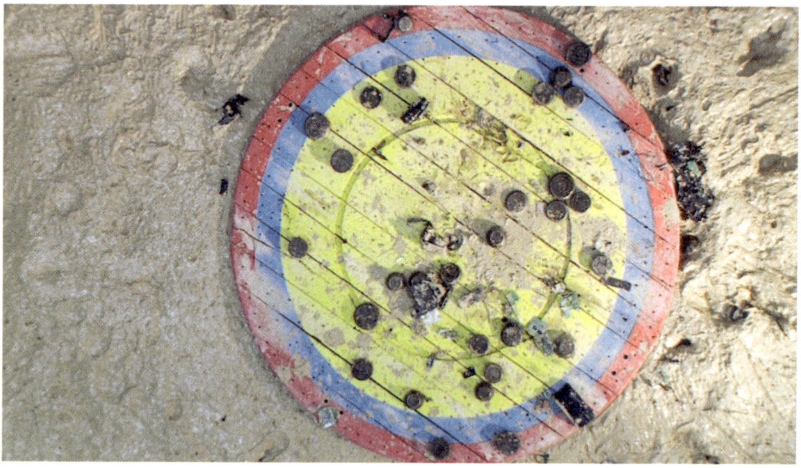

Mecha (Fuse), 2010 (video still)

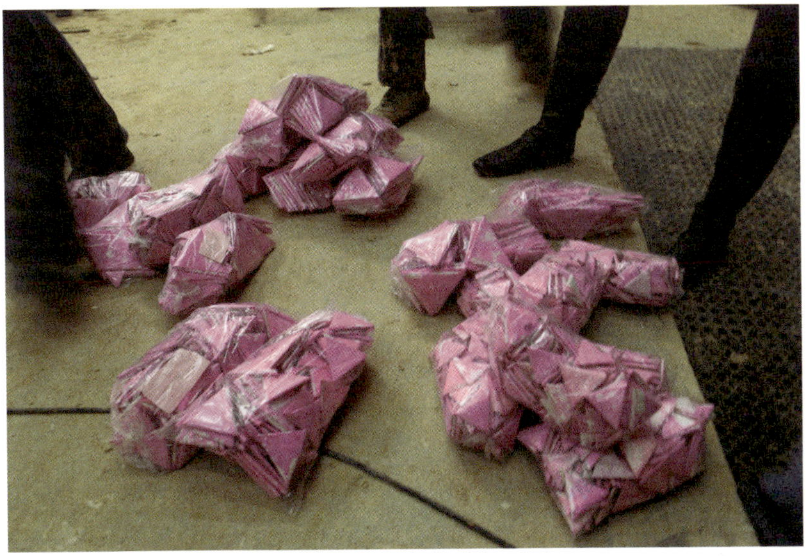

Mecha (Fuse), 2010 (video still)

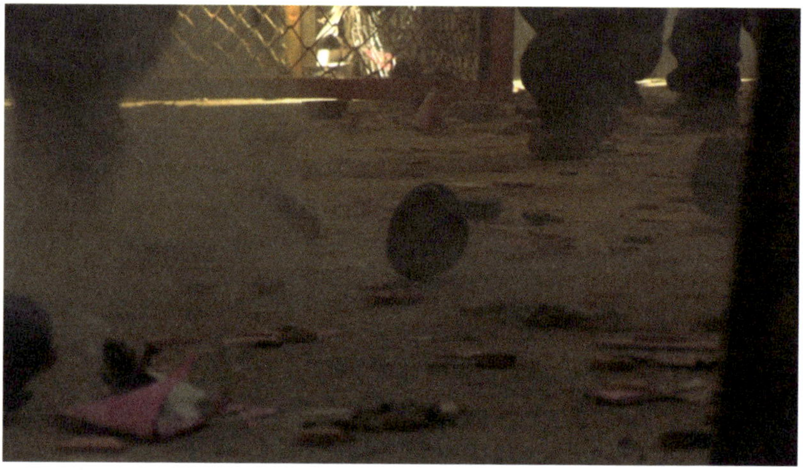

Mecha (Fuse), 2010 (video still)

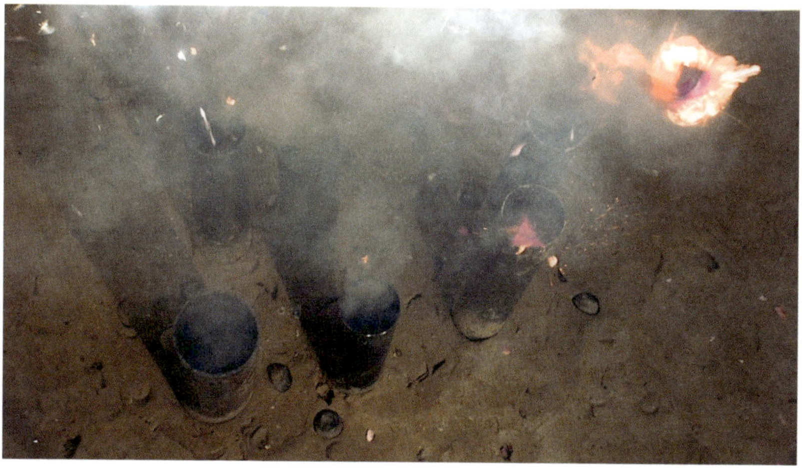

Mecha (Fuse), 2010 (video still)

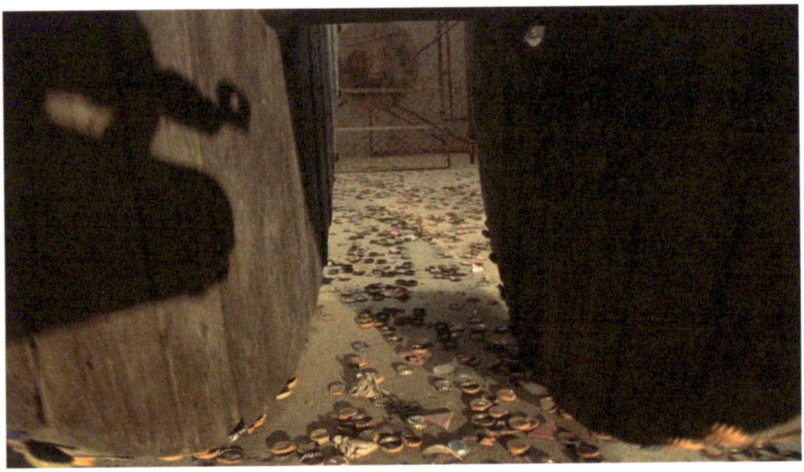

Mecha (Fuse), 2010 (video still)

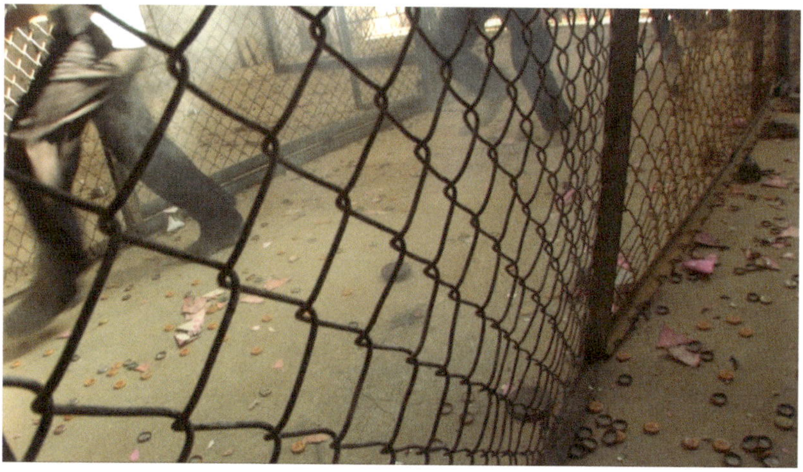

Mecha (Fuse), 2010 (video still)

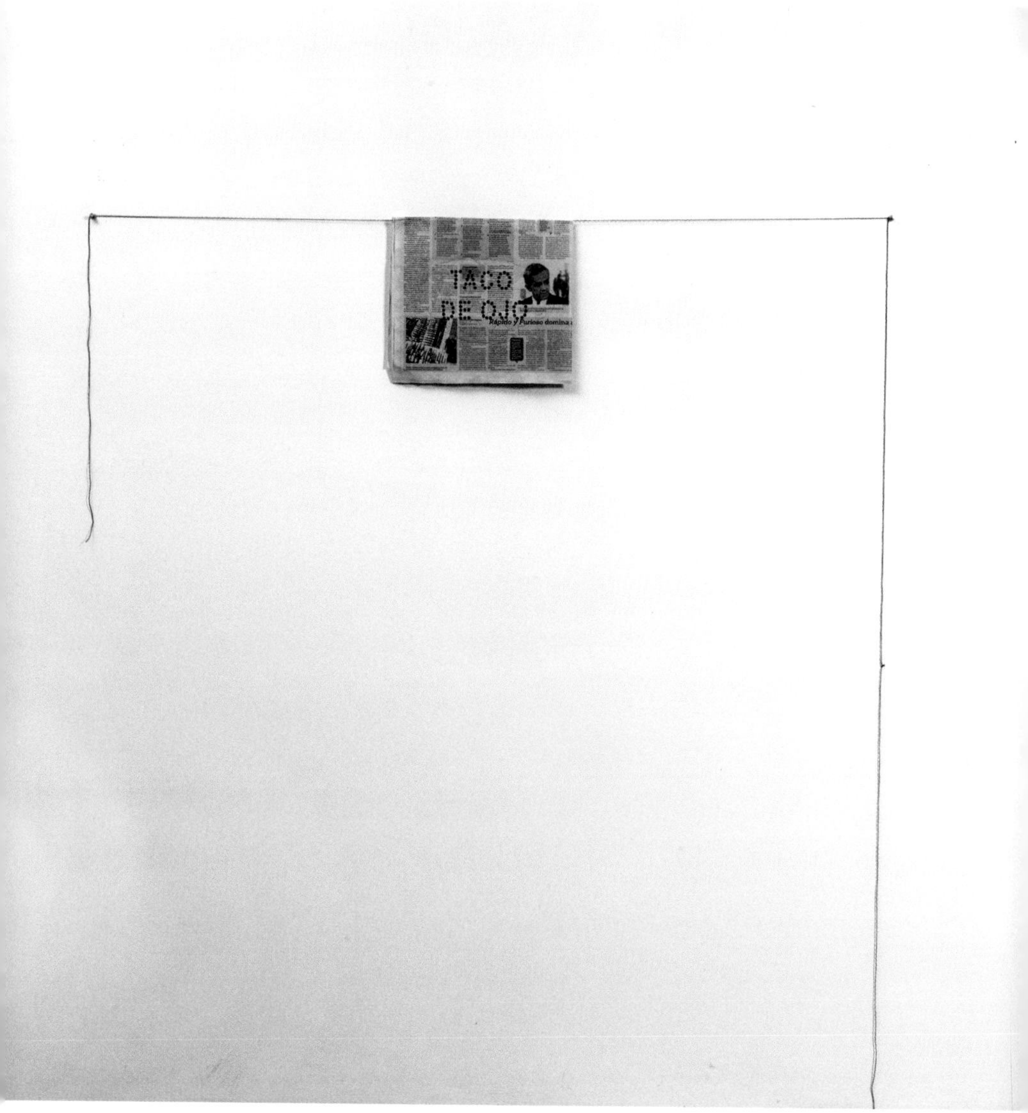

Taco de ojo (Eye Candy), 2011

Untitled (Cut Out Drawing, Medium), 2011

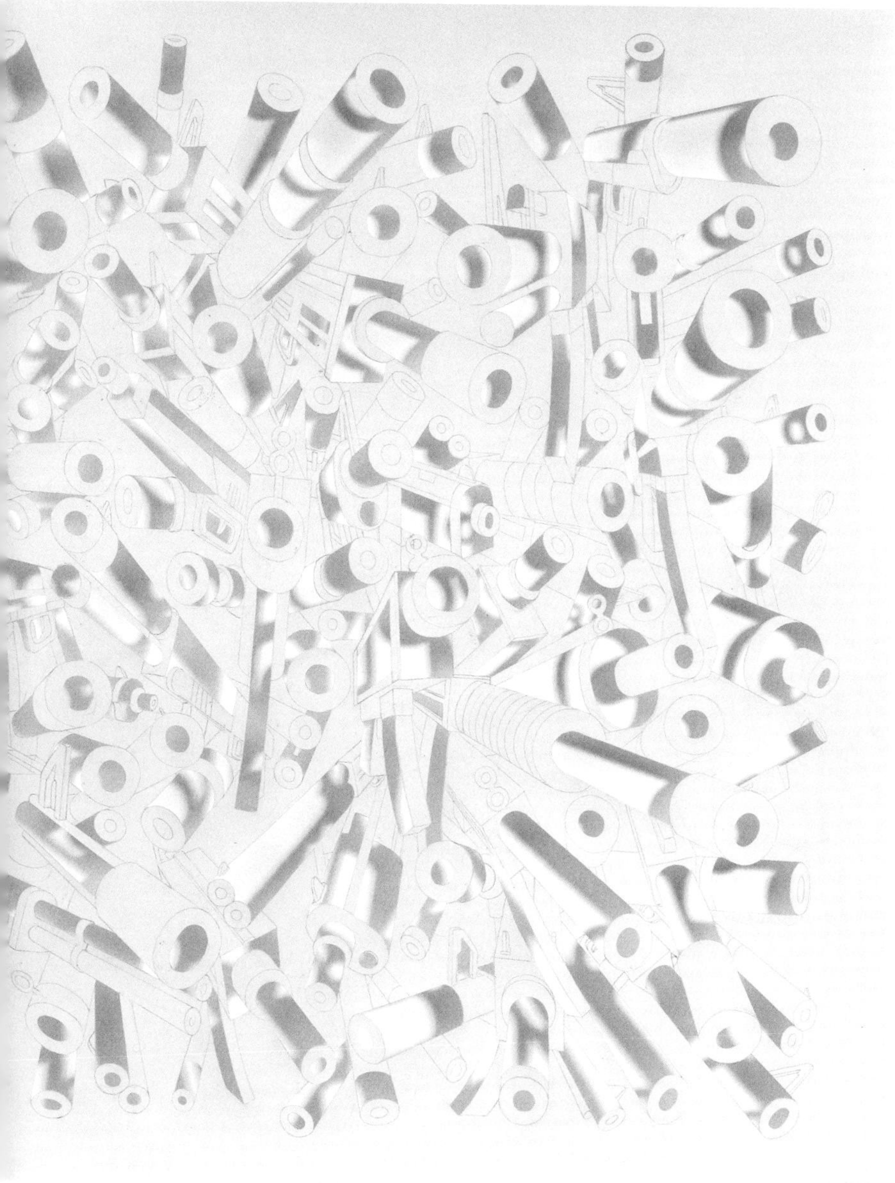

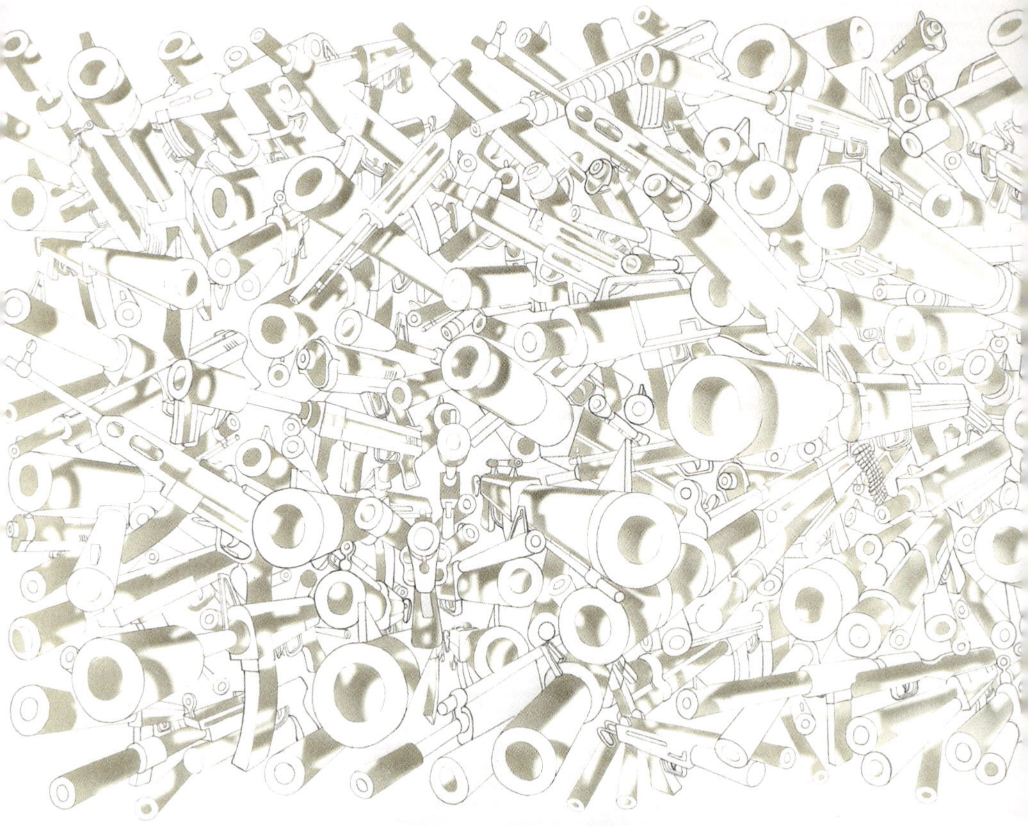

Untitled (Cut Out Drawing, Large), 2011

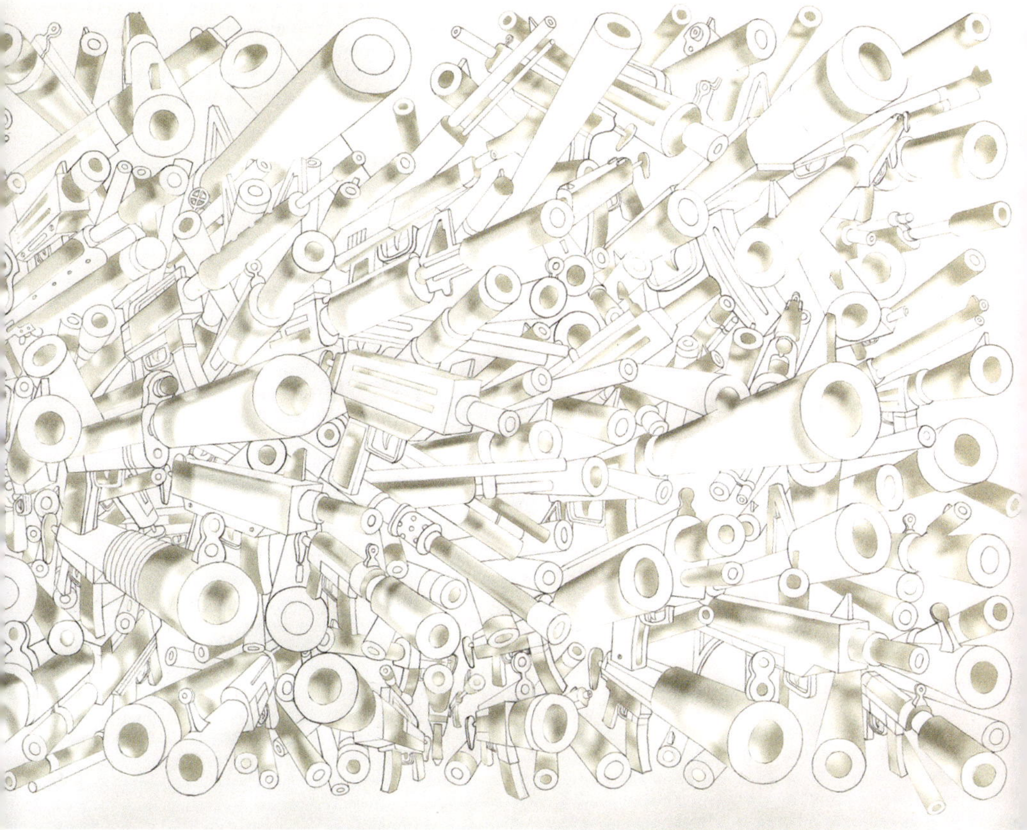

exhibition checklist

All works courtesy of the artist unless otherwise noted.

Video and sound installations

Los niños brotan de noche
(The Children Spring Forth from the Night), 2002
Single channel DVD projection
Running time: 3:30 minutes
Collection of Jimmy and Leonora Belilty, Miami, Florida

Ni me busques ... No me encuentras
(Don't Look For Me. . . You Won't Find Me), 2002
DVD, Three channel synchronized projection
Running time: 8:10 minutes
Collection of Bernardino and Mary Arocha, Houston, TX

Meta (Goal), 2009–2010
Sound installation
Running time: 8:51 minutes

Mecha (Fuse), 2010
DVD, Two channel synchronized projection
Running time: 10:02 minutes

Rooom, Rooom, 2010
DVD, Single channel projection
Running time: 3:03 minutes

Paintings

Ni me busques ... No me encuentras
(Don't Look For Me ... You Won't Find Me), 2003–2005
Oil on Formica
Eight: each 5 x 20 3/4 inches
(13 x 53 cm)

Ni me busques ... No me encuentras
(Don't Look For Me ... You Won't Find Me), 2003–2005
Oil on board
Twelve: each 5 x 20 3/4 inches
(13 x 53 cm)
One: 10 1/4 x 41 3/8 inches
(26 x 105 cm)

Drawings

El viaje del botanista
(The Botanist's Journey), 1997–2002
165 drawings, cut paper, fax paper, c-print photographs
Installation, 10 x 36 feet (3 x 11m)

Ni me busques ... No me encuentras
(Don't Look For Me. . . You Won't Find Me), 2001
Photo print
11 x 14 inches (28 x 35.8 cm)

Untitled #2 (*Meta* series), 2010
Ink on cut out paper
14 x 17 inches (35.5 x 43.2 cm)

Untitled #3 (*Meta* series), 2010
Ink on styrene with push pins
15 inches (38.1 cm)

Untitled #4 (*Meta* series), 2010
Ink on cut out paper
11 x 14 inches (28 x 35.8 cm)

Untitled #5 (*Meta* series), 2010
Ink on styrene and wood
7 x 13 inches (17.8 x 33 cm)

Untitled #6 (*Meta* series), 2010
Ink on styrene and wood
12 x 20 inches (30.5 x 50.8 cm)

Untitled #7 (*Meta* series), 2010
Ink on cut out paper
11 x 14 inches (28 x 35.5 cm)

Untitled #8 (*Meta* series), 2010
Wire and paper on ink
1 x 12 inches (2.54 x 30.5 cm)

Untitled (Cut Out Drawing, Medium), 2011
Paper
47 1/4 x 78 3/4 inches (120 x 200 cm)

Untitled (Cut Out Drawing,Large), 2011
Paper
59 x 157 1/2 inches (150 x 400 cm)
Collection of Jimmy and Leonora Belilty, Miami, Florida

Untitled (Meta 1/2), 2011
Print on paper and cut out (right)
13 x 17 inches (33 x 43.18 cm)

Untitled (Meta 2/2), 2011
Print on paper and cut out (left)
13 x 17 inches (33 x 43.18 cm)

SendEx Box #1, 2011
Cardboard and mixed media
6 x 10 1/2 x 3 1/3 inches
(15 x 27 x 8.5 cm)

SendEx Box #4, 2011
Cardboard and mixed media
12 1/2 x 6 1/3 x 2 inches
(32 x 16 x 5 cm)

Untitled, 2011
Cardboard and mixed media
5 1/3 x 10 1/4 x 1 1/3 inches
(13.5 x 26 x 3.5 cm)

Taco de ojo (Eye Candy), 2011
Newspaper and string
Dimensions variable

miguel angel ríos

Born in 1943 in San Jose Norte Catamarca, Argentina
Lives and works in Mexico and New York

Solo Exhibitions

2012
Miguel Angel Ríos: Walkabout, Des Moines Art Center, Iowa
Zooom! Decoding Common Practice, Art Miami 2011, Miami Beach, Florida
Los Impolíticos, EAC- Espacio Arte Contemporáneo, Ministerio de Educación y Cultura del Uruguay, Montevideo, Uruguay

2011
Mecha, Alonso Garces Galeria, Bogotá, Colombia
Mecha, Ruth Benzacar Galeria, Buenos Aires, Argentina
Miguel Angel Ríos: Walkabout, Museo de Arte Carrillo Gil, Mexico City, Mexico
Mecha, Nederlans Instituut voor Mediakunst, Netherlands

2010
Mecha, Galeria Millan, Sao Paulo, Brazil
Miguel Angel Ríos, Dunedin Public Art Gallery, Dunedin City Council, New Zealand

2009
Miguel Angel Ríos, Malba- Fundación Costantini, Museo de Arte Latinoamericano de Buenos Aires, Argentina
On The Edge, Museum of Contemporary Art, San Diego, California
Miguel Angel Ríos, EVO Gallery, Santa Fe, New Mexico
Maison Européenne de la Photographie – MEP, Paris, France
Crudo, Galerie Akinci, Amsterdam, Netherlands

2008
A Morir, Sala de Arte Contemporáneo, Tenerife, Canary Islands, Spain
Aquí, Fries Museum, Leeuwarden, Netherlands
Crudo, LA><ART, Los Angeles, California
White Suit, Galerie Thomas Schulte, Berlin, Germany
Distopia, Museo de Arte, La Universidad Nacional de Colombia (organized by Collection Daros- Latinamerica, Zurich and Rio de Janeiro)

2007
Aquí, Ex-convento de Tepoztlán, Morelos, Mexico
On the Edge, Marco Noire Contemporary Art (Torino, Italy), ARCO, Madrid
On the Edge, Marco Noire Contemporary Art, Torino, Italy
Fuego Amigo, Ex-convento de la Natividad, Tepoztlán, Morelos, Mexico
Aquí, EVO Gallery, Santa Fe, New Mexico
Aquí, Blaffer Gallery, the Art Museum of the University of Houston, Texas

2006–2007
A Morir, Phoenix Art Museum, Phoenix, Arizona
Aquí, Galeria Milan Antonio, São Paulo, Brazil
Concentrations 49: Miguel Angel Ríos, Dallas Museum of Art, Texas

2006
On the Edge, Jack Tilton Gallery, New York

2005
Love, Marco Noire Contemporary Art, Torino, Italy
Miguel Angel Rios, Galería de Arte Ruth Benzacar, Buenos Aires Argentina
Miguel Angel Rios, Hirshhorn Museum and Sculpture Garden, Washington, DC

2004
A Morir, Art Unlimited, Marco Noire Contemporary Art, Art Basel, Switzerland

2003
Miguel Angel Rios, Los Angeles Contemporary Exhibitions (LACE), Los Angeles, California
Miguel Angel Rios, Galerie Thomas Schulte, Berlin
Ni me busques.... no me encuentras, White Box, New York, New York

2002
Ni me busques.... no me encuentras, Basel Art Unlimited, Project Room, Marco Noire Contemporary Art, Basel, Switzerland

2001
El viaje del botanista, Sala Mendoza, Caracas, Venezuela

1999
Manhattan Códice, Museo de Arte Carrillo Gil, Mexico City, Mexico
Manhattan Códice, John Weber Gallery, New York, New York

1998
Los Vientos del Sur, Ruth Benzacar Gallery, Buenos Aires, Argentina

1995
Miguel Angel Ríos, Wohn Maschine Gallery, Berlin, Germany
Miguel Angel Ríos, John Weber Gallery, New York, New York

1993
Así en la tierra como en el cielo, Museo de Monterrey, Mexico
Miguel Angel Ríos, John Weber Gallery, New York, New York

1992
Miguel Angel Ríos, Museo de Arte Moderno, Buenos Aires, Argentina
Miguel Angel Ríos, Gallery Der Brucke, Buenos Aires, Argentina
Miguel Angel Ríos, Gallery Ramis Barquet, Monterrey, Mexico
Miguel Angel Rios: El juego y el dolor, Galeria de Arte Mexicano, Mexico City, Mexico

1991
Miguel Angel Ríos, Vrej Baghoomian Gallery Arco International, Madrid, Spain
Miguel Angel Ríos, Vrej Baghoomian Gallery, New York, New York

1989
Miguel Angel Ríos, Vrej Baghoomian Gallery, New York, New York

1988
Galeria de Arte Mexicano, Mexico City, Mexico

1984
Allen/ Wincor Gallery, New York, New York

1983
Ueda Gallery, Tokyo, Japan

1980
Ueda Gallery, Tokyo, Japan

Selected group exhibitions

2011
Unresolved Circumstances: Video Art from Latinamerica, Museum of Latin American Art (MOLAA), Long Beach, California
Essays in Geopolitics: 8th Mercosur Biennial, Porto Alegre, Brazil
Galerie Anne de Villepoix, The Armory Show, New York, New York
Universo vídeo, Historias fugaces, LABoral Centro de Arte y Creación Industrial, Gijon Asturias, Spain
Moving Image, Akinci Gallery, Art Fair of Contemporary Video Art, New York, New York
Riskzones Varldskulturmuseet, Göteborg, Sweden

2010
Les Amis de la MEP, Maison Europeenne de la Photographie Ville de Paris, France
La Trama Se Complica..., Museo de Arte Contemporaneo de Monterrey (MARCO), Mexico
No Longer Empty on the Road, Liverpool Biennial, Liverpool, England
Galeria Ruth Benzacar, ArteBa'10, Buenos Aires, Argentina
The Beauty of Distance: Songs of Survival in a Precarious Age, 17th Biennale of Sydney, Australia
20th edition of the Printemps de Septembre, Toulouse, France
Nos Meilleurs Souvenirs, Pommery Experience #8, Domaine Pommery, Reims, France

2009
Los Impoliticos, Palazzo delle Arti Napoli (PAN), Napoli, Italy
Monitaur Series, Aspen Art Museum, Aspen, Colorado
Art Video Night, Center Pompidou, Paris, France
Galerie Akinci, The Armory Show, New York, New York
For you – Para usted: The Daros Latinamerica Tapes and Video Installations, Daros Latinamerica, Zurich, Switzerland
Ringen – Group show, Cream Contemporary, Berlin, Germany
Zona de Riesgo, La Caixa Forum Madrid, Spain
Videonale, Kunstmuseum Bonn, Germany
Tiburon International Film Festival, Tiburon, California

2008
Crudo, Marco Noire Contemporary Art, Torino, Italy, Art Basel, Switzerland
Crudo, Galeria Millan, Art Basel Miami Beach, Florida
Animal Roto, Museo de Arte Moderno, Mexico City, Mexico
Zona de Riesgo, La Caixa Forum Barcelona, Spain
Atlas Américas, Rio de Janeiro, Brazil
The Last Supper Film Festival, Brooklyn, New York
Permutações Lúdicas, Pinacoteca do Estado de São Paulo, Brazil
Mediations II Biennale, Poznan, Poland

CPH:DOX (Copenhagen International Documentary Festival), Denmark
The 5th Seoul International Media Art Biennale (media_city Seoul 2008), Seoul Museum of Art, Korea
The 61st International Film Festival Locarno, Switzerland
Vijversburg VI, Friesland, Netherland
Viva la muerte, Centro Atlántico de Arte Moderno (CAAM), Las Palmas, Canary Islands, Spain

2007–2008
Face to Face: The Daros Collections (Parts 1 and 2), Zurich, Switzerland

2007
Galerie Thomas Schulte, ARCO, Madrid, Spain
Galerie Grita Insam, Vienna, Austria, MACO, Mexico City, Mexico
Fuego Amigo, 48th Festival Dei Popoli, International Social Documentary Film Festival, Florence, Italy
A Morir, Phillips de Pury & Company, New York, New York
Frontera Incierta, ERA, Montevideo, Uruguay
Counterpoint, Space*C, Coreana Art and Culture Complex, Seoul, Korea
Aquí, PhotoESPAÑA2007, Matadero Contemporary Art Space, Madrid, Spain
Allusive Moments, Rena Bransten Gallery, San Francisco, California
Outlook, Palazzo Bricherasio and Marco Noire Contemporary Art, Torino, Italy
Constructing a Poetic Universe: The Diane and Bruce Halle Collection of Latin American Art, The Museum of Fine Arts, Houston, Texas

2006
Shift, Galerie Grita Insam, Vienna, Austria
Programa de Mano, Plataforma 06, Puebla, Mexico
Festival "Printemps de Septembre – Toulouse. Toulouse, France
Polemos. Fortezza di Gavi, Gavi, Alessandria, Italy
Love, Marco Noire Contemporary Art, ARCO, Madrid, Spain
Ecce Uomo (33+1 artisti contemporanei da collezioni private). Spazio Oberdan, Milan
The Big Scene. Bregenzer Kunstverein, Bregenz, Austria
Play Forward. 59th Locarno International Film Festival, Locarno, Switzerland

2005–2006
Artgames – Analogien zwischen Kunst und Spiel, Ludwing Forum fur Internationale Kunst, Aachen, Germany
Marco Noire Contemporary Art, San Sebastiano, Torino, Italy
The Pantagruel Syndrome, T1 Torino Triennale Tremusei, Torino, Italy

2005
Marking time: moving images, Miami Art Museum, Miami, Florida
Eco: Arte Contemporáneo Mexicano, Reina Sofía Museum, Madrid, Spain

2004
57th Festival Intenazionale del film, Locarno, Switzerland
Art Unlimited, Marco Noire Contemporary Art, Art Basel, Basel, Switzerland

2003
A Morir, Artists Space, New York, New York
The Smoked Mirror, Apeejay Media Gallery, New Delhi, India

2002

Mexico: Sensitive Negotiations, Mexican Cultural Institute and General Consulate of Mexico in Miami, Florida

(The World May Be) Fantastic: 13th Biennale of Sydney, Sidney, Australia

2001

VIII Salón de Arte Bancomer, Mexico City, Mexico

The Overexcited Body: Sport and Art in the Contemporary Society, SESC Pompéia, Sao Paulo, Brazil

The Vanishing City, Programa Art Center in Mexico City & Museum of Installation in London, United Kingdom

Special Projects, P.S.1 Contemporary Art Center, New York, New York

2000

5 Continents and 1 City, Museo de la Ciudad, Mexico, Mexico City, Mexico

II festival de Arte Sonoro, Ex Teresa (Arte Actual), Mexico City, Mexico

A Selective Survey of Political Art, John Weber Gallery New York, New York

Trans Hudson Gallery, New York, New York

Exotica Incognita: Kwangju Biennale, Kwangju, Korea

Uno mas cerca al otro (Closer To Each Other): 7th Havana Biennial, Havana, Cuba

1999

The Discovery of the Amazon: Miguel Angel Ríos and Sergio Vega, CRG Gallery, New York, New York

World Views: Maps and Art, The Weisman Art Museum at The University of Minnesota, Minneapolis, Minnesota

The Third Eye, Art in General, New York, New York

Peintures et Sculptures d' Amérique Latine: Chefs d' oeuvre du XX Siécle, Museo de Bellas Artes de Caracas, Venezuela

1998

Transatlántico, Centro Atlántico de Arte Moderno, Las Palmas, Canary Islands, Spain

The Edge of Awareness, P.S.1 Contemporary Art Center, New York, New York

The Garden of Forking Paths, Kunstforeningen, Copenhagen, Denmark (Traveled to Edsvik konst & kultur, Sollentuna, Sweden; Helsinki City Art Museum, Helsinki, Finland; Nordjyllands Kunstmuseum, Aalborg, Denmark)

Amnesia, Christopher Grimes Gallery, Los Angeles, California

Terra Incognita, Centro Cultural Banco do Brasil, Rio de Janeiro, Brazil

Mesótica II, Museo de Arte y Diseño Contemporáneo San José, Costa Rica

III Bienal Barro de América, Museo de Arte Contemporáneo de Caracas Sofía Imber, Caracas, Venezuela

1997

Meditations, Madraca Ibn Youssouf, Koranic University of the XVIth Century, Marrakech, Morocco

Re-Aligning Vision: Alternative Currents in South American Drawing, Museo del Barrio, New York, New York

El Individuo y su Memoria: 6th Havana Biennial, Havana, Cuba

1996

Under the Volcano, Ex-Convento de la Natividad, Tepoztlan, Mexico

II Bienal Barro de America, Museo de Arte Contemporáneo de Caracas Sofia Imber, Caracas, Venezuela

Inclusion/ Exclusion, Reininghaus and Kunstlerhaus, Graz, Austria

Sin Fronteras, Museo Alejandro Otero, Caracas, Venezuela

1995

Dialogues of Peace, Palais des Nations, Geneva, Switzerland

Transatlántica: The America-Europa Non Representativa, Museo Alejandro Otero, Caracas, Venezuela

Mesótica: America Non-Representativa, Museo de Arte y Diseño Contemporaneo, San José, Costa Rica

Alterando Historia – Alternando Historias, Museo de Bellas Artes, Caracas, Venezuela

1994

Mapping, Museum of Modern Art of New York, New York

John Weber Gallery, New York, New York

Neo, Galeria OMR, Mexico City, Mexico

America Latina, Nuevas situaciones, nuevos proyectos, Centro de Estudios Latinoamericanos Rómulo Gallegos (CELARG), Caracas, Venezuela

Passengers, Sleeth Gallery, Wesleyan College, Buckhannon, West Virginia

1993

Museo Rufino Tamayo, Mexico City, Mexico

7 Latin American Artists, Annina Nosei Gallery, New York, New York

The Return of the Cadavre Exquis, The Drawing Center, New York, New York

Trade Routes, New Museum of Contemporary Art, New York, New York

1992

Americas: Expo 92, Pabellón de Andalucía, Convento de Santa Clara, Moger, Spain

1er Bienal del Barro de America, Museo de Arte Contemporáneo de Caracas Sofia Imber, Caracas, Venezuela

Trienal, Museo Rufino Tamayo, Mexico City, Mexico

Galeria OMR, Mexico City, Mexico

John Weber Gallery, International Contemporary Art Festival (NICAF), Yokohama, Japan,

Detour, America's Society, New York, New York

1991

The New Latin American Artists, Arnold Herstand Gallery, New York, New York

Reclaiming the Spirit, Vrej Baghoomian Gallery, New York, New York

The School of the South, Archer M. Huntington Art Gallery, The University of Texas at Austin, Texas and Reina Sofia Museum, Madrid, Spain

1990

Grids, Vrej Baghoomian Gallery, New York, New York

The Grid: Organization and Idea, Ben Shahn Art Gallery, William Paterson College, Wayne, New Jersey

XXIVeme Prix International d'Art Contemporain de Monte Carlo, Monaco

1989

Vrej Baghoomian Gallery, New York, New York

1987

Archer M. Huntington Gallery, The University of Texas at Austin

1980

Gallery Ueda, Tokyo

1979

Black Thoughts, Pratt Institute, New York, New York

Bibliography

2012

Vicario, Gilbert, ed., with Ruth Estevez, Julieta Gonzalez, Raphael Rubinstein, and Osvaldo Sanchez. *Miguel Angel Ríos: Walkabout*. Exhibition catalog, Des Moines Art Center, 2012.

2011

Gómez-Haro, Germaine. Review of *Miguel Ángel Ríos: Deambular(Walkabout)*, curated by Gilbert Vicario, Museo de Arte Carrillo Gil, September 18 - December 31, 2011. *La Jornada* (October 23, 2011). http://www.jornada.unam.mx/2011/10/23/sem-haro.html.

2010

Verlichak, Victoria. "Miguel Ángel Ríos at MALBA-Colección Costantini." *Art Nexus*, no. 75 (December – February 2010). http://www.artnexus.com/Notice_View.aspx?DocumentID=21057.

2009

Choksi, Neha. "Miguel Angel Ríos: Crudo." *X-TRA Contemporary Art Quarterly*, vol. 11, no. 3 (Spring 2009), p. 43.

Devine, John. "North Looks South at the Museum of Fine Arts, Houston." *Glasstire.com*, September 22, 2009. http://glasstire.com/2009/09/22/north-looks-south-at-the-mfah/

Klaasmeyer, Kelly. "Quick Pick." *Houston Press* (August 13, 2009). http://digitalissue.houstonpress.com/publication/index.php?i=20927&m=&l=&p=5&pre=&ver=swf

Fairfield, Douglas. "Miguel Angel Ríos: A Dangerous Cartography." *The Santa Fe New Mexican* (March 27, 2009).

2008

Trice, Emilie. Exhibition review, "Miguel Angel Ríos: Crudo." *Artforum.com* (July 21, 2008). http://artforum.com/archive/id=20781.

Miles, Christopher. "Miguel Ángel Rios at LAXART." *LA Weekly* (August 13, 2008). http://www.laweekly.com/art+books/art/art-around-town/19402/

2007

Sánchez, Osvaldo. "(un)Trade(d) Marks." in *Constructing a Poetic Universe: The Diane and Bruce Halle Collection of Latin American Art*. Beverly Adams, ed. The Museum of Fine Arts, Houston and Merrell Publishers, 2007. Pp. 100, 272-73; ill. 104-105.

"Miguel Angel Ríos." *C Photo Magazine* number 4. Ivory Press: 2007. Intro p. 9, Portfolio p. 185-195.

Fielder, Garland. "Miguel Angel Rios Blaffer Gallery." ART LIES, issue 55. http://www.artlies.org/article.php?id=1523&issue=55&s=1

2005

Henninger, Petra. "Bis zum umfallen!" *Artnet.de* (July 29, 2005). http://www.artnet.de/magazine/reviews/henninger/henninger07-29-05.asp.

Martens, Anne. "Review: Miguel Angel Ríos." *Flash Art* (January–February 2005).

Rubinstein, Raphael. "A Serious Game." *Art in America* (July 2005), p. 170-1.

Bustamante, Jean-Marc. *Lignes Brisées / Broken Lines: Printemps de Septembre á Toulouse*, vol. 3, p. 48-49.

Esmailzadeh, Karina. *artgames: Analogien zwischen Kunst und Spiel*. Exhibition catalog. Shanghai Duolun Museum of Modern Art, Shanghai. p. 36-37.

2003

Abrams, R.B. "Project Space: Morir ('til Death)." *art for real* (September 12, 2003). http://www.sitefour.com/artforreal.org/reviews_main.php?r_id=57.

Angeline, John. "Miguel Angel Rios." *Art Nexus*, Issue 49 (June – August 2003). http://www.artnexus.com/Notice_View.aspx?DocumentID=9867

2001
Rubinstein, Raphael. *Polychrome Selected Art Criticism: 1990–2000*. Hard Press Editions, 2001, pp.199-203.

2000
Helguera, Pablo. "The Discovery of the Amazon." *Art* Nexus, Issue 34 (November – January 2000).
Medina, Cuauhtémoc. "El ojo breve." *Reforma* (July 12, 2000), Cultura, 4.

1999
Gonzalez, Julieta. "Manhattan Códice." *Atlántica Internacional Revista de las Artes*, no. 24 (November 1999).
Smith, Roberta. "Art in Review: Miguel Angel Ríos and Sergio Vega." The New York Times (July 9, 1999).http://www.nytimes.com/1999/07/09/arts/art-in-review-miguel-angel-Ríos-and-sergio-vega.html

1998
Cameron, Dan. "Facing Territory." *Trans>*, issue 5.
Lebenglik, Fabián. "Los Usos y Husos del mapa." *Plástica* (November 1998), pp. 12.

1994
Rubinstein, Raphael. "The Khipus aand Maps of Miguel Angel Rios." Art Nexus, Issue 12 (May July 1994).

1987
Barnitz, Jacqueline. *Latin American Artists in New York Since 1970*. Exhibition catalogue. Archer M. Huntington Art Gallery, University of Texas at Austin.

1985
Castle, Frederick Ted. *Art in America* (May 1985).

1984
Tibol, Raquel. "La pintura sígnica de Miguel Ángel Rios." *El proceso*, Mexico DF (July 1984).

1983
Castle, Frederick Ted. *Miguel Angel Rios*. Exhibition catalog. Gallery Ueda, Tokyo.

1980
Yusuke, Nakara. *Paintings of Miguel Angel Rios*. Exhibition catalog. Gallery Ueda, Tokyo.
Paternosto, Cesar, "Miguel Angel Ríos. A personal commentary", in *Paintings of Miguel Angel Ríos*. Exhibition catalog. Gallery Ueda, Tokyo.

acknowledgments

I would like to thank Miguel Angel Ríos and his studio assistant Enrique Huerta Tovar for their extreme generosity, technical assistance, and careful attention to detail along every aspect of this project. It has been a pleasure working with them on this exhibition and publication. A special thanks to the catalog contributors: Ruth Estévez, Julieta González, Raphael Rubinstein, and Osvaldo Sánchez, who each made a substantial and long-overdue contribution to the scholarship on Miguel Angel Ríos. A heartfelt acknowledgment to Ruth Estévez and Itala Schmeltz for allowing me to present this exhibition at the Museum of Contemporary Art Carrillo Gil in Mexico City this past fall.

At the Art Center, I would like to thank Jeff Fleming, director, for his continued support and encouragement; Mickey Koch, associate registrar, for her professionalism and enthusiasm; Jay Ewart, chief preparator, for his logistical and technical prowess; Jill Featherstone, museum education director, for her creativity and enthusiasm for the subject matter; and Christine Doolittle, marketing director, for her attention to detail and tireless effort in getting the word out.

A special thanks to Jimmy and Leonora Belilty of Miami, Florida, and Bernardino and Mary Arocha of Houston, Texas, for their willingness to loan key works to my exhibition. A final thanks to Annabel Wimer, catalog designer, for deftly arranging image and text into a beautifully designed publication.

Gilbert Vicario
Senior Curator, Des Moines Art Center